the narrowest stripes possible for use on cotton, was recently used by Kotaro Shimizu (pp. 80-85) in making a sample of his work for the City of Tokyo's collection of outstanding works of craftsmanship.

THE ENDURING CRAFTS OF JAPAN

人間国宝
伝統工芸

THE ENDURING CRAFTS OF JAPAN

33 Living National Treasures

photographs by
TSUNE SUGIMURA

text by
MASATAKA OGAWA

introduction by
TSUNEARI FUKUDA

foreword by
GORDON B. WASHBURN

A WEATHERMARK EDITION
WALKER/WEATHERHILL
New York/Tokyo

This book is also published in
Japanese by Bijutsu Shuppan-sha,
Tokyo, under the title shown in
characters on the present title page—
Ningen Kokuho : Dento Kogei
(Human National Treasures:
Traditional Handicrafts). The
English text has been translated and
adapted for Western readers by
Ralph Friedrich and Miriam F.
Yamaguchi.

FIRST EDITION, 1968

Published by JOHN WEATHERHILL, INC., of New York and Tokyo,
with editorial offices at 7-6-13 Roppongi, Minato-ku, Tokyo.
Distributed in the Far East by JOHN WEATHERHILL, INC.,
and in the United States by WALKER AND COMPANY,
720 Fifth Avenue, New York, N.Y. 10019.

LCC CARD NO. 68-15702

CONTENTS

FOREWORD

by Gordon B. Washburn

This pictorial record of thirty-three Japanese craftsmen in their workshops—all artists whom the State has honored with the title of Living National Treasures—moves us both to joy and sadness. The photographs are direct and sensitive, carrying us straight into these serene workrooms where even the silence of a lacquer cutter's corner seems to be a visible thing. In their concentrated faces, whether they are weaving a basket or pouring a casting, their thought, as they lean towards their work, is nearly tangible. What more can a man want, one thinks, than to be so relaxed and so absorbed? And to have the fruit of such peaceful concentration worthy of it, unlike the anxiety of the stockbroker or the hard worries of the ad man. . . .

Looking at the lovely photographs of these quiet artists, one finds oneself sitting in their places, living their lives for a brief moment, the sunlight streaming onto one's shoulders through an open shutter or blandly filtered over one's work by a *shoji* screen. Even in empathy, we can feel what it would be like to be a dedicated craftsman; and it feels like a different world.

Alas, a different world it is, and this is the cause of the sadness. For it is a world that has nearly wholly passed away, and which only a few treasured mortals still inhabit. Perhaps their surviving crafts already suffer from the dwindling of the demand for them, tending even now towards rigidity in their decline. Yet, whether truly great or merely coldly perfect, they are but splendid survivals of a whole world of craftsmanship that the factory has doomed to extinction.

Only in such conservative lands as Japan do any such traditional crafts still live in the hands of professionals. In the West, in contrast, most crafts have moved into the leisure hours of laymen, where they survive in a badly mutilated and crippled state. Such crafts as sword forging, kettle casting, and lacquer work are, perhaps fortunately, beyond the skills of amateurs in any country.

It is useless to mourn the destructive changes that the world endures, yet one cannot help but be saddened by the increasing rarity of such artists, their beautiful tools, and their workmanship, even if one cannot ask the clock of life to be turned back or to stand still. There is, however, no harm in knowing our loss or in keenly feeling it, just as this book offers us the chance to do. It cannot be said that any one of us has made an individual choice of the machine world in place of the world of hands, but we are in the late period of such a cultural development and we have the right to be conscious of it—at least in such a fashion as this touching and delicate volume allows.

INTRODUCTION

by Tsuneari Fukuda

Even in this highly materialistic age we often like to tell ourselves that material things are basically of little or no importance, although most of us, if we are being strictly honest, will admit to a passionate interest in them. When we are in a philosophical mood, we tend to say that mind is more important than matter or that the spiritual excels the material. At the bottom of this way of thinking, however, is the mistaken notion that the spiritual and the material are in opposition to one another. In fact, we elaborate this mistaken notion into the concept of idealism versus materialism, and of course it is always idealism to which we attribute the greater virtue. Actually, though, there is no major difference, for the ideal is often expressed in the material, and the worshiper of ideals can be just as dangerous as the worshiper of material things.

When we say of something that it is only a "thing"—only a lifeless object—we are thinking of the dominant position of the spirit, but I wonder if we really believe the spirit is that important. If we treasure the spirit so much, it would seem to be our own spirit and not that of others. That is to say, we are concerned with ourselves but not truly concerned with others; we recognize our own spirit, but other people are merely objects. In a purely literal sense, of course, no one can actually endow an object with spirit (although, as this book makes clear, the hand-created works of man do have a spirit of their own), and thus, if we treat others as nothing more than objects, we do not credit them with having a spirit and are therefore being no more than hypocrites ourselves.

An injunction sometimes ascribed to Confucius states that when we make light of people we lose virtue, and when we make light of things we lose strength of will. Those of us who pretend to despise material things disrespect the spirit of others and treat them as objects, thereby losing the very virtue we seek to gain. On the other hand, material things should represent a means of communicating the human spirit, and, in fact, it cannot be communicated more effectively by any other means.

Not only the living national treasures who appear in this book but all craftsmen who work with their hands have instinctively understood this immutable truth. They have, so to speak, annihilated themselves in their service to material things, controlling whatever selfish feelings they may have had and devoting themselves to bringing out the spirit in the objects they have created. It may well be that, at the beginning, such objects were "just things" even to them, that the objects were not yet "alive" and thus could not speak out. The only way, then, that they could make these stubbornly silent objects speak out was to devote themselves selflessly to the act of creation.

In fact, there is no other way. Purely mechanical creation, with absolute control of the material and the resulting product, implies no true respect for that product, since no thought has been given to endowing the product with a character and a spirit of its own. Nor have the materials themselves been credited with individual character and spirit. The true craftsman—and by this is meant the craftsman who works with his hands—knows that the material he works with has a mind of its own and that if he seeks to impose absolute control, both the material and the finished product will take revenge upon him. To be sure, the materials of craftsmanship are willing to be controlled if their special qualities and virtues are understood and appreciated, but they do not openly reveal the nature of their adaptability. This is for the craftsman to discover, and when he meets with the refusal of his materials—and consequently of his creations—to adapt themselves absolutely to his preconceived demands, they become, for the first time, living objects to him. As for those of us who are attracted by the products of his craftsmanship and do not look upon them as mere mechanical creations, the more we treat them as living objects, the more fluently they begin to speak to us and, one might say, understand our feelings.

The relation between the maker and the product should also be able to exist between the product and the user. The importance of the artisan spirit and the handiwork lies precisely here, and it is neither nostalgia for the more leisurely and non-mechanical past nor the desire to perpetuate an anachronism—the men and women who create with their hands in a day when the machine is practically omnipotent—that impels one to say this. It has always been true, and it remains true today. Otherwise, why should we grant more prestige to excellent handmade objects than to those which tumble out of machines by the thousands? Nowadays we are surrounded by the uniform creations of mass production, all of them quite dead, and even while we take advantage of the handiness of these non-alive things, we still look down upon them for the dead things that they are. And at the same time we suffer from this, for there is no communication between these spiritless objects and ourselves. Usually we do not recognize the reason for our peculiar dissatisfaction with the products of the machine, for we think of them in a purely utilitarian sense, and it rarely occurs to us that there is an estrangement between them and us. And yet the pleasure we find in handling and drinking from a handmade pottery teacup, for example—the sense of communicating with it in some indescribable way—instantly reveals the source of our unconscious dissatisfaction with mass-produced things. The pottery teacup, we instinctively feel, has a life of its own, a spirit with which no machine on earth could infuse it, and we experience a peculiar delight in its company. What is important, then, is that both the craftsman and the user of his products regard these creations as living objects—objects to be made with love, treated with affection, and used with care. This is the only way to restore the man-to-man relationship that should exist between maker and user by way of the created object.

There could hardly be a finer demonstration of this truth than the present photographic study. Tsune Sugimura and his camera have visited and intimately observed thirty-three of Japan's living national treasures in the craftsman category, and the results speak for themselves. It is plain to see that he was deeply impressed by the importance of these craftsmen and their creations, that he wished them to be more widely known, and that he listened to their silence (for, after all, there is a silence about such creation) through the lens of his camera. The enthusiasm and the honesty that he displays in this book are qualities that he holds in common with the craftsmen themselves, and no qualities could be more appropriate in a man who wishes to introduce the living national treasures among the craftsmen of Japan to the wider audience they deserve.

THE ENDURING CRAFTS OF JAPAN

by Masataka Ogawa

The characteristics of Japanese art as a whole are reflected in the minor arts of Japan, for the same creative spirit that produced the great sculpture, the great painting, and the great architecture of the country pervades all levels of artistic production. It is deeply rooted in the everyday life of the Japanese people and may well be called unique. Although, in the minor arts, it cannot express itself on a monumental scale, it is there nevertheless, and it accounts for the high esteem in which the products of traditional Japanese craftsmanship have always been held, first by the Japanese themselves and more recently by Westerners as well.

When the artist Joan Miró visited Japan and was escorted to Kyoto and Nara to see the treasures of classical art and architecture, I noted that he was more interested in the industrial arts and handicrafts than in the painting and sculpture. During his tour of the Katsura Detached Palace several carpenters were engaged in repairs, and he was much more curious about the traditional tools they were using than about the architecture and the garden for which the palace is celebrated. At the famous Shigaraki kiln in Shiga Prefecture he was most attracted by an old piece of pottery set up in the front yard of a potter—especially by the natural cracks in it and the way the glaze had been dripped upon it. He admired the simple sense of beauty that characterizes the Japanese: their ability, as he expressed it, to reflect the beauty of nature in their crafts and, in particular, their delicate sensitivity toward materials. He was most impressed by the skillful teamwork of a father and son who were shaping a large piece of pottery on the wheel and was quite touched, he said, by the magical work that the Japanese produced with their hands.

Many similar incidents could be cited to illustrate the great attraction that Japanese handicraft products hold for visitors from the West. The skill displayed by Japanese craftsmen in the use of their hands has a certain wizardry about it that is sometimes almost beyond our imagining. To be quite honest, we Japanese are proud of the skillfulness of our hands, but it is not only because of our ability to do minute work. The hand must be creative as well as adept. The scholar Nyozekan Hasegawa* has aptly stated that Japan is a country of the "culture of hands." This culture of hands, he points out, can also be seen in the crafts of ancient Greece, but there the craftsmen were not actually Greek citizens themselves but slaves acquired through military conquest. Even Aristotle, he notes, regarded these craftsmen as something like animals ranking between human beings and cattle. In Japan, on the other hand, outstanding artists and craftsmen have been highly respected since ancient times. We all know well, as Mr. Hasegawa explains, that painters, sculptors, swordsmiths, and carpenters were given honorary titles and that, as can be seen in scroll paintings picturing old-

* The names of all modern (post-1868) Japanese in this book are given, as in this case, in Western style (surname last); those of premodern Japanese, in Japanese style (surname first).

time craftsmen, they wore costumes not unlike those of the court nobility as their working uniforms.

It is the world of the industrial arts in Japan that most significantly displays the culture of hands. In fact, the word "hand" itself in Japanese has always been symbolic of manual skill as well as manual labor, of special ability as well as natural strength, and this concept of the "hand of the Japanese" is an integral part of the daily life of the people. In one of his essays Mr. Hasegawa calls attention to the great number of expressions in Japanese, both standard and colloquial, that employ the word "hand"—that is, *te*—to embody a special concept of action, ability, or skill. Among such expressions we may note *te ga agaru* (to improve in one's skill), *te ga tarinai* (to be shorthanded), *te o nuku* (to omit the necessary steps), *te o mawasu* (to send out emissaries), *teate* (medical treatment), *teuchi ni suru* (to kill a person with one's own hands or to strike a bargain), *te o hiku* (to withdraw oneself), and *te o dasu* (to meddle with, to turn one's hand to, to make advances to). There are also such words as *katarite* (narrator) and *yarite* (an able man), in which the word "hand" stands for the possessor of a particular skill. In a word, the Japanese language, no less than Japanese culture, is saturated, so to speak, with this concept of the hand.

✦

The history of the Japanese represents a process of constant improvement in the status of the common people. In ancient times the classes were distinctly separated, and a small aristocracy ruled over a mass of commoners that included slaves. During the Heian period (794–1185), when Japanese culture reached one of its great peaks, the nobility, centering around the court and the powerful Fujiwara family, lived in luxury and monopolized a highly developed culture which the common people had no privilege of sharing. The warrior class of this period existed only to protect the aristocracy. In the Kamakura period (1185–1333), however, the warrior class stood on equal footing with the nobility, and during the succeeding Muromachi (1333–1568) and Momoyama (1568–1600) periods a number of commoners rose to warrior status, thus strengthening the position of the ordinary populace. In the Edo period (1600–1867) the populace became so influential, both economically and intellectually, that no political administration could be undertaken without considering its aspirations and desires.

Needless to say, these changes in the social structure of Japan were clearly reflected in the history of the industrial arts. The craft products that had earlier been elegant and chic, and often even effete, to please the tastes of a small aristocracy, gradually became more robust and, at the same time, more wholesome under the influence of popular demand. For the industrial and handicraft arts, such changes in the social structure were invigorating, since the privileged class had tended more and more to require meaninglessly elaborate products for the sake of maintaining its special status and had altogether ignored the tastes of the commoners. Later, of course, even among the commoners, there developed tendencies to demand increasingly elaborate craft products—for example, some of the overornate decorative screens of the Momoyama and Edo periods—and thus it cannot be said that the social changes invariably produced a healthful atmosphere for the development of the handicraft arts. Nevertheless, when we consider the long history of craftsmanship in Japan, we find that in general the hands of the Japanese expressed naturally the "life feeling" of the people—their delicate affection toward their own daily living.

Perhaps the most significant characteristic in the history of Japanese craftsmanship is the recurrent demand for simplicity and candor in handicraft products. While it is true that the clay figures and the earthenware of the Jomon period (from around 4000 to about 200 B.C.) are more elaborate than similar works of the later Yayoi period (about 200 B.C. to about A.D. 250), they are far simpler in decoration than the bronzes of the nearly contemporary Yin and Chou dynasties of China. I have no intention of passing judgment on the superiority or inferiority of ancient Japanese and Chinese craftsmanship, but I think it is interesting, nevertheless, to find such widely different concepts of beauty between these two Oriental civilizations. The well-known *haniwa* mortuary figures of Japan's Yayoi period are all of a clean and wonderfully naïve quality. The same may be said of the curved jewels called *magatama,* which evidently copied the animal claws from which primitive men made necklaces and other personal adornments. This simple and honest form is in striking contrast with comparable Chinese jewels which attempted to copy the forms of animals themselves. To call attention to this fact is not to imply an invidious comparison but merely to point out that simple and straightforward forms have always had an immense appeal for the Japanese.

✦

The German architect Bruno Taut feels that he has found in Japanese art a quality that distinguishes it from the art of all other countries: a flow of line, as he describes it, a lightness of skill, a certain serenity—a cheerfulness, even—that reflects the tranquil character of the artist and is perhaps the most outstanding feature of Japan's artistic achievement. To sum this up in a single word, Mr. Taut calls it purity, and he considers it no exaggeration to say that it characterizes the whole treasury of Japanese art.

It would be difficult, however, to make this generalization apply to the entire range of Japanese art or to all the products of the handicraft arts. For example, the five-stringed lute among the treasures in the Shoso-in, the eighth-century storehouse at Nara, is anything but simple in its mother-of-pearl decoration, and the ornate metalwork found on ancient mirrors and incense burners is far from naïve. In fact, these objects are hardly less than gorgeous. It is true that many of the Shoso-in treasures show the influence of T'ang China and even of examples of Greek and Persian craftsmanship that found their way to Japan as early as the eighth century. It cannot be said, however, that the treasures of craftsmanship in the Shoso-in, even though made by Japanese hands, reflect the true life feeling of the people of that time. It was only gradually that the gorgeousness of such products was refined by genuine Japanese sensitivity into the elegant beauty that characterizes the best of Japan's art—a spirituality, one might say, that had its origin in Buddhism and the concept of *mono no aware,* which may be literally translated as "the sadness of things," the "sadness" here implying a sensitivity to beauty that one is at a loss to describe. This new concept of quiet elegance that entered Japanese art as T'ang influence waned was first fostered by the aristocracy and only later penetrated to lower levels of society. There were periods, of course, when the Japanese reverted to overdecoration in the arts and crafts, but eventually restraint always reasserted itself.

The rise of the warrior class in the twelfth century stimulated the handicraft arts to new activity. In principle, the military rulers of the Kamakura period discouraged the luxurious way of life that had been followed by the nobility of the preceding Heian period and had, in fact, led to their downfall. A modest and much more vigorous style of living became the order of the day. Regardless of the Spartan injunctions of the government, however, arms and armor became increasingly decorative, and the talents of swordsmiths and other craftsmen were prodigiously employed. In the succeeding Muromachi and Momoyama periods—that is, from the mid-fourteenth to the close of the sixteenth century—this tendency in the handicraft arts continued to grow, and architecture and painting eventually followed suit. It was an age of castle building, as well as of almost incessant civil war, and all the decorative arts were called into service. For sheer gorgeousness, we are told, the Jurakudai palace of the military dictator Hideyoshi and his castle at Fushimi (both in Kyoto) had never been equaled. We are even told that a teahouse built by Hideyoshi in Kyoto was "all made of gold." Unfortunately none of these fabulous structures have survived, although there is no reason to doubt their magnificence.

As an example of the general trend toward luxury, we may note that even in Kamakura times the use of both gold and silver in lacquer decoration gave way to the exclusive use of gold, and the possibilities of imposing decorative design were more widely explored. Although during the Muromachi period there was a retreat to more delicate techniques, the Momoyama period brought a new outburst of extravagance in lacquer art. Daring designs and striking color combinations were used to produce the showy effects that became the hallmark of the age. The arrival, in the mid-sixteenth century, of the first Westerners ever to reach Japan stimulated the urge toward the exotic in all the decorative arts.

The decorative sense of the Japanese people thus fluctuated between quiet elegance and almost unrestrained exuberance. Nevertheless, a harmony was achieved, and often, strangely enough, the simple and the elaborate were effectively brought together in a single composition. A famous Noh robe of the Muromachi period illustrates this rather paradoxical achievement. Half of the front is red, half black, and this arrangement is repeated in the back. The black sections are decorated with arabesques and designs of clematis, the red with large leaves and folding fans. The combination of contrasting ground colors is simplicity itself, but the decoration is undeniably ornate. And yet the effect is harmonious, and the impression is one of quiet strength and elegance.

This same daring sense of design is reflected in a Momoyama lacquer box in the collection of the Kodai-ji, a temple in Kyoto. Here each side is divided into two sections of black and beige and decorated with powdered gold—the black areas in a design of bamboos, the beige in a design of autumn grasses. Again, decorative contrasts have created an engaging harmony. It is this peculiar sensitiveness of the Japanese toward the boldly ornamental on the one hand and the exquisitely simple on the other that makes the handicraft arts of Japan unique.

The sense of tranquility and purity that Bruno Taut has found in Japanese art and craftsmanship is of course a notable characteristic. I would rather speak of it, though, as an elegant simplicity. And this elegant simplicity has much to do with the religious philosophy known as Zen, the form of Buddhism introduced from China in the Kamakura period. Zen had a tremendous appeal for the warrior class of Kamakura times, and its dedication to the beauty of simplicity had a profound influence on the handicraft arts—an influence which at times may seem to have waned but which persisted nonetheless.

Along with Zen came the custom of drinking tea, first as a religious and then as a social function. Although tea had been introduced from China during the Nara period, the Japanese did not develop a passion for it until the Kamakura period, when the Zen priest Eisai reintroduced it. Now tea drinking became the rage, and all sorts of developments followed. Some of these, it must be admitted, were far from the simplicities of Zen. There was, for example, a game called *tocha,* a name which might literally be translated as "battle of tea." The contestants were required to drink various brews of tea and then to guess where the tea had come from, and the winners were regaled with luxurious gifts or sumptuous dinners. Small wonder, then, that tea parties often turned into bouts of gambling or that those who gave the parties sought the utmost in tea utensils and equipment. Needless to say, the handicraft arts were willing to answer the needs.

In the succeeding Muromachi period, however, all of this changed, and tea drinking as a social event became formalized into *chado* (or *cha-no-yu*), the tea ceremony as we know it today. The shogun Ashikaga Yoshimasa, enamored of the soberly refined art of Sung China, set the tone of Muromachi elegance, and it was under his influence that the tea ceremony developed as a distinctive feature of Japanese culture. Among Yoshimasa's protégés was the tea master Shuko, who formulated the canons of *chado,* the new idea in tea drinking. The essence of this cult of tea, as it is often called, was the same elegant simplicity that I have spoken of before. Ostentation was to be avoided at all costs, and true refinement was to be expressed in the unpretentious and the plain—even to the use of peasant tea bowls from Korea for drinking the ceremonial beverage. It goes without saying that the other utensils and the tearoom itself were required to be equally unpretentious, and the atmosphere of the tea party, although not solemn, was spiritual and serene—a far cry, indeed, from some of the tea parties of Kamakura days. This concept of ceremonial tea, of course, is followed in the tea rituals of today, and to be a *chajin,* a master of tea, is to command respect, even from those who are not initiates of the cult.

Again, as in Kamakura times, the cult of tea encouraged the creativeness of Japanese craftsmen, particularly the potters and the makers of iron teakettles. It was not until the Muromachi period, in fact, that the teakettle was recognized as a handicraft product worthy of artistic attention. Iron, of course, was the plainest of metals and thus could not violate the canon against ostentation in the tearoom. Its texture harmonized with that of the pottery tea bowls, and when it was wrought into kettles of simple but pleasing shape the effect was exactly right. Thus under the influence of the tea ceremony the humble kettle won great respect.

The tea bowls were naturally the main accessories, but they were allowed to be no more decorative than the teakettle or the tearoom itself, which is to say that they were not decorative at all, at least not in the sense of calling attention to themselves through brilliance of color and mechanical perfection of form. Sobriety of color was the keynote, and absolute symmetry of shape was never an obsession. The more rustic, in fact, the better, and any suspicion of artifice was to be condemned. Such wares as Raku, Shino, and Oribe were highly prized—sometimes incontinently so, with the result that celebrated tea bowls often changed hands at prices that are still breathtaking today.

Recently the Japanese word *shibui* has come into use in other languages to express the concept of elegantly restrained beauty that is typified by the tea ceremony and its accessories. It is fitting that the word originated in tea itself. It was first used to define the taste of the green tea called *shibucha*—not a simple taste that could be readily described as mild or bitter but something more complicated and somehow more meaningful. At the first sip, the taste of *shibucha,* as anyone who has drunk it will quickly agree, is a good deal less than pleasant, but the more one drinks, the better it seems to become. The word *shibui* is often used to describe colors, designs, and forms, and what it really means is difficult to say in simple terms. The essence of it, though, is a certain serenity and depth of meaning: the qualities that are found in the finest products of Japanese craftsmanship—the qualities, in effect, which infuse these products with the creative but disciplined spirit of their makers and somehow give them a life of their own.

It can be seen, then, that the traditional arts and crafts of Japan reflect a uniquely Japanese sense of beauty and that an essential element of this beauty is the harmony of what at first may appear to be disparate parts. The best place to appreciate this harmony of disparity, as we may call it, is a tearoom. Here the painting hung in the tokonoma (decorative alcove), the simple flower arrangement, and the unpretentious utensils of the tea ceremony—all individually beautiful and each worthy of undivided attention—come together in a unity of greater dimensions, so to speak. Each object has its place in a broader and more spiritual design.

As another example of this interesting harmony of disparate parts, we may note that the primary attraction for foreigners at a Japanese meal is usually not the food (which, in fact, often disappoints them) but the beauty and variety of the dishes in which it is served. At the usual Western dinner party all the dishes, from soup to dessert, are of the same pattern and shape. They most unmistakably belong to a set, and any dish that happens to be different is viewed as an intruder. At a Japanese dinner party, however, no such concept exists, and lacquer, porcelain, and pottery vessels appear in a multiplicity of designs, colors, and shapes. Each has its meaning and purpose, depending on the food that is served in it, and one surprise follows another as the various courses reach the table. Often the whole ensemble appears at the same time, and the array may be astonishing indeed. But to the practiced eye the harmony is evident, and it does not take long for the sensitive novice to discover it. One reason for this harmony of diversity is that the dishes are credited with what one might call an identity of their own—an identity conferred by the hand of the craftsman and not to be submerged by making everything conform to one material, pattern, and shape. Together they express the spirit of the craftsman himself, who created them with affection and thereby added a certain touch of richness to what would otherwise be the most routine of objects.

Of course I am speaking ideally here, for I am thinking of true craft products and not the spiritless products of the machine. Nevertheless, the products of the machine have largely taken over in Japan during the past one hundred years. Ceramics, weaving, and dyeing, to name but a few of the traditional crafts, have long since become chiefly the province of mass production by machinery, and the handicraft arts, which were once responsible for all of Japan's production, now occupy only a small part in our lives. A certain disharmony has thus entered the world of harmonious beauty in which the Japanese lived until about a century ago. Although industrial design in Japan has improved greatly since the end of the Pacific War in 1945, we are still in a state of spiritual confusion over the change to mass production. No thoughtful Japanese is willing to relinquish the past entirely, and hardly a one of us will deny the superiority of handmade craft products to the products of the machine. But the products of the human hand are increasingly rare and increasingly expensive, and sooner or later we have to compromise.

Because of the strong pressure that the machine has exerted on almost every aspect of our daily life, the hand of the Japanese craftsman—that hand which once created every object we lived with and often deeply loved—has fewer and fewer opportunities to display its marvelous skill. It would be no exaggeration, I believe, to say that Japanese aesthetic life has thereby been placed in peril.

It was in this belief that the Japanese Ministry of Education, in 1950, established a unique system for the protection of traditional arts and crafts that stood in danger of vanishing from the scene. The performing arts as well as the handicraft arts were to enjoy this protection, and men and women who had mastered the skills of these arts and crafts, thereby keeping them alive, were to be honored by being designated as "holders of important intangible cultural properties." The Japanese public, however, has little patience with the stilted language of bureaucracy and, by analogy with those works of art and architecture which are officially designated as "national treasures," has long since taken to calling these respected men and women "living national treasures." And that, of course, is exactly what they are.

It will not be out of place here, I think, to give a brief résumé of the system by which these living national treasures are chosen. Ever since 1871 the Japanese government has had a system for preserving ancient works of art and architecture and other "tangible legacies" by designating them as either national treasures or important cultural properties. In 1950, under the Cultural Assets Protection Law, this system was regularized and extended to include "intangible legacies" as well. The traditional theater, traditional music, traditional dance, and traditional crafts all come under this "intangible" category, and so it happens that the living national treasures include actors as well as potters and a Noh drummer as well as a maker of iron teakettles. Of the men and women who have been honored in this fashion since the first appointments were made in 1954, fifty-two are still alive—nineteen in the performing arts and the thirty-three representatives of the handicraft arts who are included in the present book.

As the system now works, administered by the Ministry of Education, living national treasures are nominated periodically by the Ministry, whose nominations are then acted upon by a committee of private citizens made up of experts in the field, including scholars, craftsmen, critics, museum directors, and the like. The criteria used in making the selection are: 1) that the handicraft itself be worthy of protection, 2) that the craftsman be outstanding for his techniques, 3) that the craftsman and his work be of a stature to deserve a place in the history of Japanese craftsmanship, and 4) that special emphasis be placed upon the preserving of regional crafts. Designation as a living national treasure, though in the main an honorary distinction, somewhat similar to the knighting of outstanding artists in England, also carries with it a small yearly stipend, averaging about one thousand dollars, to be used principally for the training of younger practitioners of the craft.

In the handicraft arts the purpose of the living national treasures is not only to preserve significant traditional techniques but also, by their activities, to encourage the creation of new techniques suitable to the demands of the present day. It is not easy, however, to make the roots of tradition put forth branches that will flower and bear fruit in an overwhelmingly mechanical age. Although the superb skill of the traditional craftsman's hand is still displayed today, the problem is how to transfer the spirit of the handicraft arts to the machine. In a word, how can the mass-produced creations of the machine be made to reflect the enduring traditions of Japanese craftsmanship? On the face of it, the problem may seem to be insoluble, but I have the feeling that a solution can be found. And when it *is* found, the products of the machine will also add a dimension of pleasure to the everyday living of the Japanese people. The hands of the Japanese, which created and served the traditions of craftsmanship over thousands of years, cannot remain idle at a time when the machine is threatening to eclipse their work forever.

陶芸

THE ART OF THE POTTER

Since the sixteenth century, when Japanese porcelains first found their way to the West, Japan has been famous as a country of ceramics. Long before that time the art of the potter had been elevated to a high position among Japanese handicrafts, and an amazing variety of ceramic types had been developed. The fame of modern Japanese pottery is no less bright than that of the wares produced in earlier times, and the number of foreigners coming to Japan to study ceramic techniques has increased constantly since the Pacific War. To discover the secret of Japan's renown in ceramic art, it is necessary to look back into history—quite far back, I should say—and to review the achievements of several thousands of years. It is necessary, also, to look at the Japanese themselves as they expressed their exceptional, and sometimes unpredictable, aesthetic sense in their ceramic creations.

The ceramic art of Japan dates back to the Stone Age, and its earliest known products are those of the Jomon (rope pattern) type, so called because they are decorated with designs made by impressing the wet clay with straw ropes, and the grotesque earthen images known as *dogu*. Both the Jomon vessels and the *dogu* express the imagination and energy that were to characterize Japanese ceramics in almost every period of later history.

In the succeeding Yayoi period, when a metal culture began to replace that of stone, ceramic techniques underwent a remarkable change, and a greater sophistication was achieved. At this stage we already find the potter's wheel, and we know that his wares were fired at a higher temperature. The Yayoi pottery, far less decorative in concept than that of the Jomon period, displays a simplicity and conciseness of shape and design. And thus, even in prehistoric times, we can note the two tendencies that were to serve as fundamental poles in the later development of Japanese art: the exuberantly decorative and the elegantly simple.

Influences from the Asian continent were at work in Japan at least as early as the fourth century of the Christian era, and the import of Korean techniques, in particular, can be observed in the ancient pottery known as Sue ware. During the Asuka (552–710) and the Nara (710–94) periods, as Chinese and Korean influences became stronger, the manufacture of glazed pottery began. Ceramic development during the Heian period (794–1185) appears to have made no great advances, if we are to judge by the few surviving examples from that time, but the advent of the thirteenth century brought a new outburst of creative energy. A greater variety of glazes came into use, and the resulting diversification of wares expressed an ever widening range of imagination. Among the famous wares that came into production at this time were those of the Seto region along the northern coast of the Inland Sea. Trade with China during the fourteenth and fifteenth centuries introduced new and stimulating influences, and it was not long before the Japanese were learning the techniques that had produced the celadons and the white and off-white porcelains of Sung and Ming, as well as the *temmoku* tea bowls that were to become a passion with tea-ceremony addicts.

In the brief but wonderfully creative Momoyama period (1568–1600) the decorative arts of Japan reached a climax of exuberance, and a remarkable array of new ceramic types appeared. Foremost among the patrons of the arts was the military dictator Toyotomi Hideyoshi, whose tastes set the tone for the times. Among his protégés was the potter Chojiro, whose tea bowls so charmed the dictator that he was given permission to sign his works with the character *raku* (pleasure), which formed part of the name of Jurakudai, Hideyoshi's palace in Kyoto. Thus there came into existence the famous Raku ware of Kyoto.

Three other types of ceramic ware for which Japan became famous were born of military conflict. During the closing years of the sixteenth century, when the forces of Hideyoshi made two unsuccessful attempts to subjugate Korea, many Korean potters were brought to Japan as valued prizes of war and were established in Kyushu and western Honshu to create the wares that eventually became known as Arita, Satsuma, and Hagi.

Also about this time the potters of the Seto region introduced such new wares as Shino and Oribe, both favored for tea bowls, while the kilns of Mino (Gifu Prefecture), Bizen (Okayama Prefecture), and Shigaraki (Shiga Prefecture) made themselves renowned for the pottery that came to bear their names. A vast improvement in techniques marked the ceramic production of these kilns and many others during the Momoyama period.

The two and a half centuries of the Edo period, which began about 1600, witnessed an unprecedented flourishing of Japanese ceramic art. At Arita, in Kyushu, strong influences from Ming and Ch'ing China stimulated the production of superb porcelains, and new techniques of glazing and enameling were developed. In Kyoto these influences were to bear fruit in the masterly works of Nonomura Ninsei, who profited by the knowledge from China to create porcelains of refined and uniquely Japanese design. At the same time the introduction of new enameling techniques at the Kutani kilns in Kaga Province (now Ishikawa Prefecture) led to the production of the porcelain that was to become famous as Old Kutani.

The development of ceramic art during the Edo period embraced almost all of Japan, and production increased tremendously. It was not only the well-known kilns of long tradition that flourished. New centers of pottery making were established, and in such remote countryside regions as those of northern and western Honshu many potters who would remain unknown to history worked energetically at their humble trade, turning out large numbers of common utensils for daily living.

Although the foregoing is anything but a complete history of Japanese ceramic art in premodern times, at least the main outlines have been shown. It is clear that ceramic development in Japan during the Asuka, Nara, and Momoyama periods was strongly influenced by the importation of Chinese and Korean ideas, and the casual observer may therefore be disposed to say that the ceramic art of Japan is an offshoot of continental traditions. Yet, when we study the prehistoric pottery of Japan, we may well doubt this, and, as we shall presently see, our doubt is more than justified. But foreign influence was not limited to that of China and Korea, for influences from the West also entered Japan during the Momoyama and Edo periods. Dutch ceramics, for example, attracted Ninsei's follower Ogata Kenzan, who even tried to copy them. Their influence upon Kenzan's mature style was slight indeed, but it was there nevertheless.

Regardless of foreign influence, however, a native originality always asserted itself. Ideas from abroad were adapted in distinctively Japanese ways, and it cannot be said that Japanese ceramics are merely the mixed-blood offspring of foreign and native collaboration. Their originality lies in the inborn taste and sensibility of the Japanese, a quality that has been passed on from one generation to another down the long corridor of time. It is true that Japanese ceramics lack the intensity, as we may call it, of the creations of Sung and Ming, but on the other hand this very lack of intensity is characteristically Japanese. In other words, we find in this fact a clue to the general approach of the Japanese toward nature. To the raw clay as well as to the effects produced upon it by the fire, the Japanese have shown an attitude of gentleness and affection. Soft and simple lines and textures have always been preferred, and this quality can be noted in the long range of Japanese pottery from the works of the Yayoi period to the relatively modern creations of the Bizen potters.

Again, the Japanese paid little attention to artificial creativeness—that is, absolute mechanical perfection of shape and design. On the contrary, they appreciated the harmonious imbalances of nature and were happy when these were mirrored in their creations. It would be rare to find in traditional Chinese or Western ceramic works such asymmetrical shapes and patterns as one frequently finds in Japanese pottery. Quite often the products of Japanese kilns lack absolute symmetry, sometimes by accident, sometimes by design. If the distortion is a natural result of the firing, this is not looked upon as a failure but is appreciated as a form of beauty in its own right. And again, like the beauty of asymmetry, the natural effects produced by glaze and fire were highly admired in Japan as expressions of the mysterious beauty that only nature could create.

This attitude of respecting nature and seeking to reflect it in art could have ended up in decadence, just as the contrary penchant for artificial perfection and gorgeous decorative design might (and sometimes did) take the same road. But good sense and an instinct for balance between natural and decorative beauty usually managed to save the day, and the elegantly decorated Kakiemon vase is no less worthy of admiration than the roughly formed Raku tea bowl.

In considering the long history of ceramic art in Japan, we must not ignore the countless products of unknown potters throughout the country. There is a vast difference, of course, between their humble creations and the refined works turned out by well-known artists to please the tastes of upper-class patrons. But the everyday utensils that emerged from the kilns of these nameless artisans, although rough and stolid, have the energy and wholesomeness of folk art, and they are properly admired today for a beauty that is theirs alone. It was only half a century ago that folk pottery came to be recognized as an important phase of Japanese ceramic art. Until that time, the common ceramic items of everyday use, even though they may have given pleasure through their honesty of texture and design, were not regarded in any way as aesthetic creations. Utility was all that mattered, and, except for certain tea masters and a handful of others who could see beyond mere utilitarian purpose and discern beauty where it was least expected to be found, no one considered folk pottery as even a distant relation of more sophisticated ceramic types.

It was Dr. Soetsu Yanagi who awakened the Japanese to aesthetic values that they had come to ignore, and the folk-art movement that he initiated some fifty years ago is vigorously alive today. That the movement has encouraged the maintenance of traditions among folk potters is only one of its virtues. More important to the potters themselves is the fact that it has encouraged their survival in an age when they have been threatened more than once with extinction.

Among the many Japanese potters today who are dedicated to the preservation and further development of their craft, five have been designated as living national treasures. They are, in the order of their appearance in the following pages, Munemaro Ishiguro, who is noted for his success in reviving the metal-glaze techniques of the T'ang and Sung dynasties, once an important source of inspiration in Japanese ceramic art; Toyozo Arakawa, who has devoted himself to studies of the classical Shino and Black Seto techniques; Toyo Kaneshige, whose fascination with the textures of clay has led him into intensive research on traditional Japanese ceramic methods; Shoji Hamada, a leader in the folk-art movement who has revitalized folk-pottery production at the well-known Mashiko kilns and brought the folk-art spirit into modern Japanese ceramics; and Hajime Kato, whose studies and achievements in color decoration have won him renown. One other master of color decoration is regrettably no longer among the living national treasures. He was Kenkichi Tomimoto, who died in 1963.

石黒宗磨

MUNEMARO ISHIGURO

Explorer of Ancient Techniques

It was almost pure chance that launched Munemaro Ishiguro on his career as a potter. In 1918, as a young man of twenty-five, he saw for the first time a prized tea bowl of *yohen temmoku,* a type of old Chinese pottery in which the fire of the kiln produced constellations of iridescent spots in the jet-black glaze. He was enchanted by its lustrous texture and remarkable coloring, and he decided to discover the long-lost secret of its manufacture. He was not a potter at that time, for he had come to Tokyo from his native Toyama Prefecture to work for a shipping firm, but his fortuitous look at the *yohen temmoku* bowl turned him into a potter for life.

In 1927 he moved to Kyoto to begin his research into the ceramic techniques of T'ang and Sung China, hoping that eventually he would learn how to create *yohen temmoku* himself. So far, however, the ultimate secret has eluded him, but he has made remarkable discoveries along the way. He was able, for example, to revive the techniques that produced the three-color T'ang and Sung wares and the much admired *egorai* pottery that once served as everyday utensils in China and Korea. He succeeded also in reproducing the techniques of *mokuyo* (leaf pattern) and several other types of *temmoku.* But the rarest type of all, the *yohen temmoku* that first delighted him half a century ago, is still an unachieved goal.

Nevertheless, Ishiguro is not discouraged. The years of research have been long, but they have been productive as well. Besides, as he points out, sheer imitation is not creation, even though much is to be learned from the study of old techniques. His works are prized among collectors, and his reputation among modern Japanese ceramists is secure. It was his iron-glazed ceramics that won him the honor, in 1955, of being named a living national treasure.

✦

In the photographs that follow, we first see Ishiguro in his workshop at Yase, near the foot of Mount Hiei in Kyoto. Winters are bitterly cold here, and he uses various devices (like the covered tank in the foreground) to keep his clay and his glazes from freezing. His wintertime work must be done during the warmer hours of the day. On page 8 appears an example of the iron-glazed ceramics for which he is famous: the "thousand-spot tea bowl" in the Okabe Collection, Tokyo. On page 9 Ishiguro uses a cord to cut a newly turned bowl from the mass of clay on his wheel. In the last photograph (pages 10–11) we see him at the approach to his Yase kiln, whose name is carved on the stone post at left.

7

荒川豊蔵

TOYOZO ARAKAWA

Master of Shino and Black Seto

Even to Japanese who have only a slight interest in ceramic art, the name of Toyozo Arakawa immediately suggests two traditional wares: Shino and Black Seto. Both of these—Shino, with its thick, snowy glaze and its air of softness and tranquility, and Black Seto, with a certain solemnity about it—made their first appearance in the Momoyama period. In 1930, when Arakawa discovered an abandoned Shino kiln in his native Gifu Prefecture, he resolved to devote himself to the preservation of traditional ceramic techniques. He had begun his career as a student of painting in Kyoto. In 1922 he turned to ceramics, studying first with Tozan Miyanaga and then with the famous Rosanjin Kitaoji. His main interest during these years was techniques of coloring, but after his discovery of the old Shino kiln he involved himself almost exclusively with Shino and Black Seto.

It is no easy task to revive a ceramic tradition that has all but vanished. Arakawa established his kiln at Kuguri, in the lonely Gifu countryside, and there, after long years of effort, he succeeded in creating works of Shino and Black Seto that even surpass those of earlier times in their excellence of glaze and design. For this accomplishment he was designated a living national treasure in 1955. His recent works—tea bowls, sakè bottles, flower vases—express more than anything else a keen awareness of nature. His sensitive use of color and the dignified texture of his glazes show that he has now reached the supreme stage of his art, where he can work with fire and clay to create ceramics of astonishing beauty.

Arakawa fires his kiln only once a year. This means, in effect, that he spends more time creating his works in his mind than he does in actually producing them. He works in a genuinely rural setting, and his pottery has a distinctly rustic air: a clear reflection of his great love for nature and his humility in its presence.

✦

In the facing photograph, Arakawa shapes a bowl on the wheel. The wooden tool in his hand is a throwing stick, which he uses to help form the contours of the piece. The Shino tea bowl on page 14, from the collection of Koichi Nakanishi, displays not only great beauty of glaze and design but also a characteristically Japanese asymmetry. On page 15, Arakawa examines a tea bowl that he has just removed from the wheel. His workshop (pages 16–17) is no less rustic than its natural surroundings. Here, with his typical concentration and skill, he puts the finishing touches to a tea bowl before taking it from the wheel. Like the one at the right, it will clearly bear the marks of his hands: the deliberate distortions that give it the desired asymmetry.

金重陶陽

TOYO KANESHIGE

Potter of Bizen

Toyo Kaneshige was born to the ceramic art. His father was a master potter of Bizen, the area in Okayama Prefecture where kilns were founded as early as the Kamakura period to produce the pottery that was to become famous as Bizen ware. It was Kaneshige who was to bring this ware to new life in the twentieth century.

The clay of the Bizen region is rich in iron, and it is this quality that gives Bizen ware a texture and hardness suggestive of metal. The potters of Bizen customarily used no glaze, although they produced decorative designs in the ware by draping it with ropes of rice straw which, as they burned in the fire of the kiln, left curving lines of red on the dark surface. The subdued color, the natural texture, and the quiet simplicity of Bizen pottery commanded the admiration of masters of the tea ceremony, and the ware enjoyed great popularity from the end of the Muromachi period to the early Edo period. From around 1830, however, it began to display a certain sterility of inspiration, and its popularity declined.

The man who stimulated the ceramic art of Bizen to new and vigorous achievements was Toyo Kaneshige. He began by making an intensive study of Old Bizen, the ware produced during the earliest days of the Bizen kilns. His research into types of clay and firing processes eventually enabled him to create pottery in the great Bizen tradition, and for this achievement he was named a living national treasure in 1956.*

There is an air of dignity and strength about Kaneshige's Bizen pieces that is somehow reminiscent of the warriors of old. Deeply rooted in the best of Bizen traditions, they are decidedly masculine in concept and design. In a word, they express the essence of the Bizen clay itself.

✦

On the opposite page we see the sensitive hands of Kaneshige at work on a large Bizen plate, his fingers creating the pattern in the clay. The workshop scene on the next two pages is of particular interest because of the role that his wife plays in the production of his wares. Her function is to help turn the wheel, and to people who are rash enough to suggest the use of a mechanical wheel he says: "The trick of my work lies in turning the wheel rather irregularly, and this device of having two people do the turning makes for much more interesting shapes." The Kaneshige jug on page 22 is fully emblematic of his work: sturdy and virile and suggestive of ancient times. In the last photograph of this section (page 23) we see the raw material of Kaneshige's creations: the blocks of hard Bizen clay that are brought to his kiln from the surrounding region.

* Toyo Kaneshige died at Okayama, aged seventy-one, on November 5, 1967, shortly after the Japanese edition of this book had been published and during the preparation of the English edition. But his contributions to the world of Japanese ceramics will long endure.

浜田庄司

SHOJI HAMADA

Folk Potter

Someone once asked Shoji Hamada if he wasn't bothered about his numerous imitators. "Not in the least," he replied. "In a hundred years or so, all their best pieces will be taken for mine, and my failures will be taken for theirs." This straightforward and tranquil philosophy is typical of the man who now stands first among the folk-art leaders of Japan.

Hamada's career in ceramics, which covers more than half a century, has included a variety of significant undertakings: a three-year sojourn in England, where he worked in close association with the celebrated potter Bernard Leach; a lengthy stay in Okinawa for the study of native pottery; other visits abroad, including some for the purpose of teaching; and a prodigious amount of activity in Japan's folk-art movement. But it was his move to Mashiko, in Tochigi Prefecture, in the 1920's that proved most significant of all, for there he indisputably came into his own as a ceramic artist of the highest rank.

Mashiko had for some time been a center for the production of pottery for everyday use: teapots, tea bowls, jars for bean paste, and the like. Hamada was attracted by the pure and vital quality of the Mashiko clay and the charming naïveté of its products. He saw here an opportunity to express in his own work the basic virtues of folk art displayed in the work of the anonymous Mashiko craftsmen: honesty, fortitude, and vigor. It was in acknowledgment of his contribution to folkcraft ceramics that he was named in 1955 as a living national treasure.

Hamada's style is unmistakably his own, but it is deeply rooted in Mashiko traditions. It is masculine, forthright, and bold, and those who know his work can never be taken in by mere copies of it. Small wonder, then, that he is not in the least troubled about his imitators.

✦

In the first of the photographs that follow, firewood for Hamada's kiln is stacked outside his imposing traditional-style farmhouse in Mashiko. On the following two pages (26–27) we see Hamada himself in characteristic good humor. Visitors, of which he actually has far too many, are always received with a hospitality that is astonishing in such a tremendously busy man. In the next photograph (pages 28–29) Hamada shapes the mouth of a bottle on the wheel. The eloquence of his hands requires no comment at all. The strong and resolute bottle-vase on page 30, with its gray ash glaze and its faintly brushed pattern, expresses the perfection of Hamada's art. On the following four pages (31–34) we see, first, a firing door in his kiln; second, part of the main entrance to his house, with three clay paddles above, a wooden slab bearing his name at center, and a plate with his telephone number below; third, his favorite working place, with his sitting cushion in front of his wheel; and last, a detail of his kiln, with its tile roof and its round smoke vents.

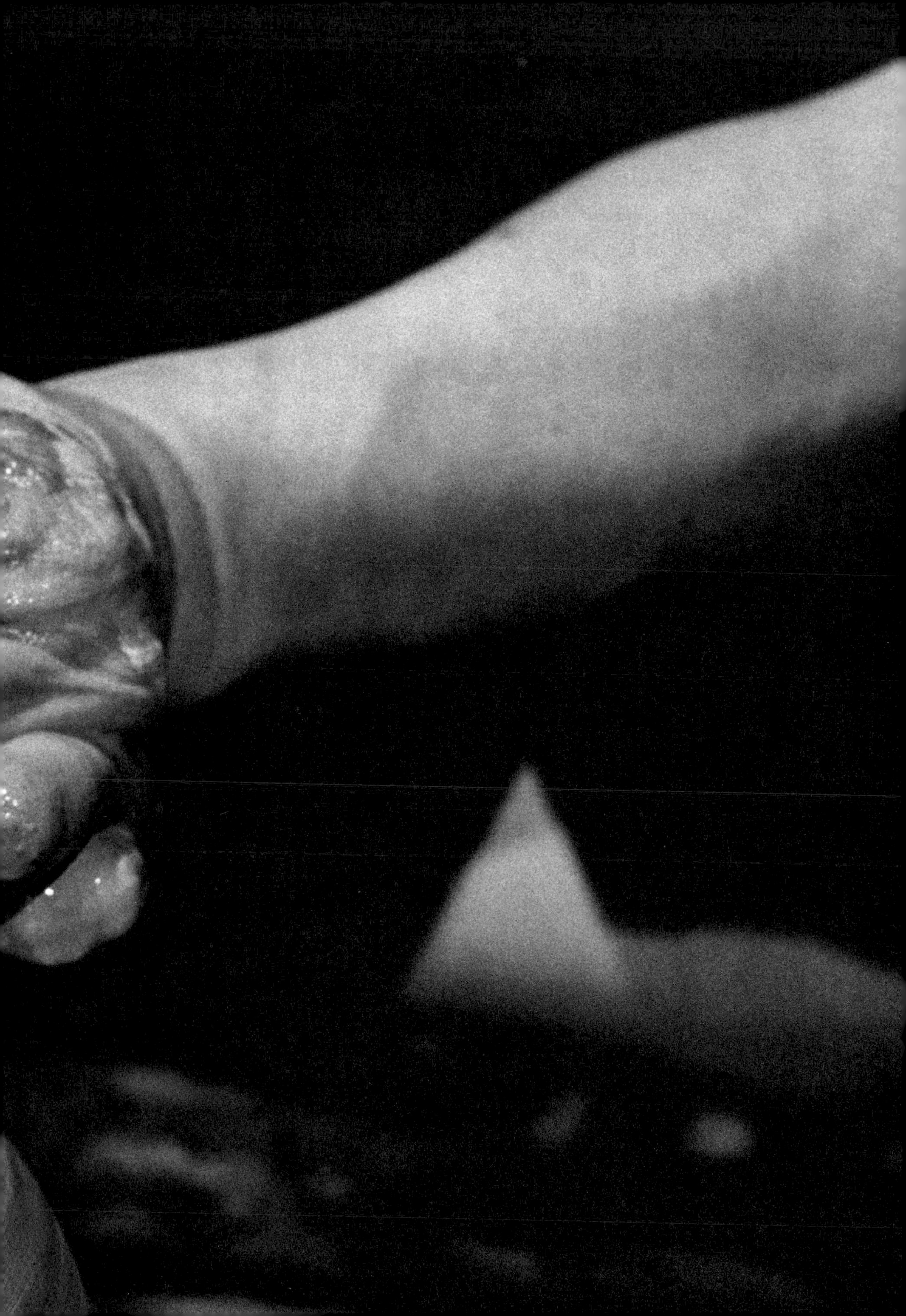

電話
36
益子

加藤土師萌

HAJIME KATO

Master of Color

Perhaps the best word for the elegantly turned and exquisitely decorated works of Hajime Kato is "aristocratic." In fact, it was his mastery of color decoration that won him nomination as a living national treasure in 1961. Considering his constant emphasis on the "mental sense" of the potter and the way this is reflected in his work, one might be tempted to call him an intellectual among Japanese ceramists. His renown as a technician is great, but sheer mastery of technique has not been allowed to obscure creative imagination in his works, nor has it been stressed to the detriment of human feeling.

Kato was born in the ceramic ambience of Seto, but his first inclination was toward painting. Ceramic design, however, seemed to offer a better chance for earning a living, and in 1939 he constructed a kiln in Yokohama and has been established there ever since. Originally his style was rather rough and plain, but this gave way in time to a much more sophisticated statement of his talent. His ceaseless experimentation with color techniques led him to a mastery of such processes as those that produced some of the finest works of Ming-dynasty China, and these, infused with his own creative spirit, are frequently displayed in his work.

Kato is a perfectionist, but he has the utmost patience with his students and with other young potters who besiege him for criticism of their work. He invariably finds time to answer their questions and furnish advice. "No ceramic artist," he says, "can attain excellence without intense concentration and complete sharpness of mind. Technique is important, but keen mental awareness is the most important of all."

✦

The first of the following group of photographs shows Kato painting an overglaze design of carnations on one of his newly fired bowls. The magnificent sakè cups on page 38, from the collection of Makio Isono, are decorated on the outside with an intricate pattern of chrysanthemums in gold with varying ground colors and on the inside with a floral design in traditional blue-and-white. They are marked on the bottom with the artist's seal. On page 39, Kato molds a tea bowl, using his fingertips to create a pattern of ridges in the clay. Page 40 shows four steps in the turning of a tea bowl, from the start with a lump of kneaded clay to the finished bowl after it is removed from the wheel. On page 41, Kato demonstrates (top to bottom) the shaping of larger pieces: hand-molding a bowl before turning, using a wooden scraper to form the contours of a wide bowl, creating a bulge at the upper rim of a bowl, and shaping the top of a large vase. The plate on page 42, intended as an ornament and decorated with branches and blossoms of the flowering plum on a mottled dark-blue ground, is representative of the superb coloring techniques for which Kato was named a living national treasure. Like the sakè cups on page 38, it is from the Isono Collection.

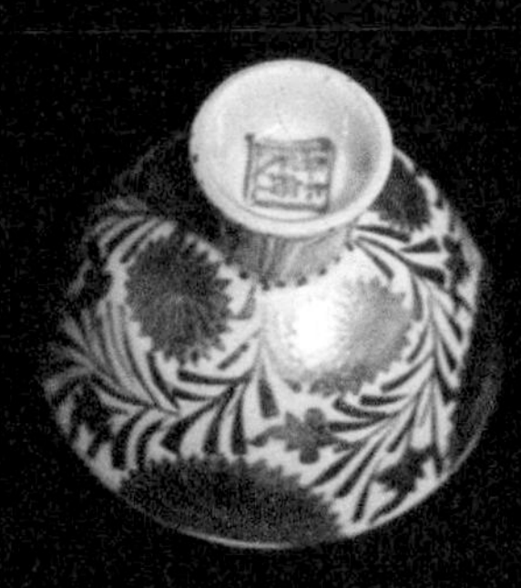

染織

THE TEXTILE ARTS

Japan's prominence in the textile arts has long been acknowledged. Ever since the handicraft creations of Japanese weavers and dyers first reached the West, they have commanded no less admiration there than in Japan itself. The advent of the modern age, although it has brought large-scale machine production of fabrics formerly made entirely by hand, has not completely vanquished the textile craftsmen who still produce the finest of Japan's fabrics. The chief reason for the craftsmen's survival is the continuing Japanese fondness for the traditional kimono, which is most prized when it is made of hand-loomed and hand-dyed cloth. Among the textiles still woven by hand are the linen of Niigata, the pongee of Ibaraki and Tochigi, and the various silks of Kyoto. In the dyeing of fine fabrics, Kyoto is supreme, for it has been the center of this craft for centuries. A number of cotton textiles are also hand-loomed even today, since they are in demand for summer kimono. In a word, the skill and good taste of traditional textile craftsmen are still appreciated by discerning Japanese.

Long before we have historical proof of the textile arts in Japan, we have indications in mythology and legend that they were given prominence in Japanese culture from the very earliest times. The sun goddess herself, reputed founder of the imperial line, was accomplished in the craft of weaving, we are told, and the legendary weaving girl who was placed among the stars with her herdboy lover is still honored with her own festival on the seventh of July. The empresses of Japan have traditionally been regarded as patronesses of sericulture and the textile arts, and the present empress is no exception.

Much of the inspiration for Japan's textile crafts came from China, as ancient legends and records both attest, but the Japanese, in their own creative way, could not long be content with the mere copying of foreign styles and techniques, and in the course of time they evolved methods of weaving and dyeing that were peculiarly their own. So it was, also, in pottery, lacquer, metalwork, and the other handicraft arts: conscious borrowing at the beginning, steady development, and eventually the emergence of a distinctively Japanese craft. It is not immodest for a Japanese to point this out, for it is no more than a statement of fact, and Western observers have long been aware that what begins in Japan with imitation often ends up as an improvement over the original. At the same time, one may well ask what civilized country has not profited by borrowing the inventions of other countries and adapting them to its own needs and tastes, adding improvements as it went along. In any event, the reputation of Japan's traditional textiles throughout the world is proof enough of their high quality. But it is time to halt this digression and to see what actual history can tell us about the development of Japan's textile arts.

The arts of weaving and dyeing appear to have occupied the hands of Japanese craftsmen at least as early as the Yayoi period (about 200 B.C. to about A.D. 250), for fragments of textiles and what are guessed to have been looms, as well as earthenware patterned with impressions of textiles made in the wet clay, have been found at prehistoric dwelling sites. It is difficult to learn much from such fragile survivals, and a great deal of guesswork has resulted. Still, it seems safe to say that textiles were among the earliest handicraft products of Japan.

The oldest written Japanese record states that around A.D. 199, during the reign of Emperor Chuai, silkworm eggs were sent as a gift from a Chinese emperor and that the son of this emperor, along with some 25,000 other Chinese, became a naturalized Japanese in the following century. With these immigrants came valuable knowledge of weaving and dyeing techniques, and subsequent migrations of Chinese and Koreans brought additional knowledge. We are told that dyeing techniques, in particular, were thus greatly improved. Fragments of silk fabrics found in Japanese tombs of the fourth and fifth centuries indicate that the techniques of textile manufacture of that time were quite a bit more advanced than those of the other handicraft arts.

It is not until the Asuka and Nara periods, however, that we can really judge the quality of Japanese textile art, and by that time—that is, from the sixth to the eighth century—it is well advanced indeed. From the Asuka period, for example, there remains a section of the embroidered hanging known as the Tenjukoku Mandara, a representation of the Buddhist paradise made in memory of the illustrious leader Prince Shotoku. Among the eighth-century treasures of the Shoso-in repository at Nara are stunning examples of textiles like *aya* (a type of silk damask), *nishiki* (silk brocade), and *ro* (a gauze-weave silk) that indicate a remarkable proficiency in weaving and dyeing techniques. Japanese dyers of the time were well acquainted, for instance, with the batik and tie-dye processes.

The dyeing of the Heian period (ninth to late twelfth century) developed the Nara-period techniques toward greater perfection, and certain new techniques were introduced. Textile patterns changed from the large and colorful to the small and elegant. The elaborate court costumes of women called for more subtle dyeing processes, particularly in the "layered" ensemble known as the *juni-hitoe:* garments of graduated size and delicately varying color worn one over another to create a rainbow effect at the edges. Ceremonial dress for men similarly demanded more sophisticated weaving and dyeing techniques.

The Kamakura period (thirteenth to mid-fourteenth century), which saw the rise of the warrior class, placed more emphasis on practicality than on decoration in clothing, and the technical level of weaving and dyeing was somewhat lowered as a result. In the following Muromachi period, however, a new stimulus to the textile crafts accompanied the reopening of trade with China, and Japanese weavers learned the techniques of producing such fabrics as *kinran* (gold-patterned silk), *donsu* (silk satin damask), and the striped material known as *kando.* A flourishing textile industry developed around the towns of Sakai, near Osaka, and Hakata, in Kyushu. The growing popularity of the Noh drama during this period stimulated the development of dyeing into an extremely refined craft, and Noh costumes became increasingly gorgeous and ornate. As the period drew to a close, various foreign fabrics found their way to Japan, among them the printed cottons of Southeast Asia and the velvet of Europe, and the knowledge of Japan's textile craftsmen was much increased by such importations.

In the late sixteenth century, as the Momoyama period developed into a splendor and brilliance heretofore unknown in Japan, the textile crafts entered a new epoch of color and design. Gold was much used in costume decoration, either woven into fabric as thread or impressed upon it as foil or dust applied to wet lacquer or paste. The tie-dyeing process of *shibori* was improved to new standards of intricacy and excellence, and the entire craft of dyeing enjoyed considerable prosperity. The Noh robes and the ceremonial costumes of the period were gorgeous in the extreme. The military dictator Toyotomi Hideyoshi, patron of weavers and dyers as well as of potters, encouraged the import of Ming weaving techniques and the establishment of a production center for fine textiles in the Kyoto suburb of Nishijin—a center whose fabrics are world-famous today.

During Japan's last feudal age, the 250 years of the Edo period, which began about 1600, the textile industry of Kyoto became even more active, and this activity stimulated production in other areas of Japan. Popular demand for quality fabrics increased as the merchant class emerged into prominence, and costume design became more and more colorful and free. Government efforts to control luxurious living were usually circumvented in one way or another, and extravagance in kimono decoration often reached an outlandish level. One dyeing technique of the Edo period, however, represented a supreme achievement in the craft: the resist technique known as *yuzen,* by which designs of great delicacy and superb color—usually flowers, birds, or natural scenery—could be produced to make kimono of astonishing beauty. It is this technique which survives today as one of the most admired in kimono decoration.

The peak of brilliance in Edo weaving and dyeing was reached around the middle of the period. From that time on, sheer inventiveness in kimono decoration was no longer prized, and more sober tastes prevailed. A certain sense of freshness was perhaps lost, but the move toward decadence had at least been stopped. In the provinces, where feudal lords encouraged the growth of local handicraft industries, new textile centers flourished, and their products reflected the new taste for plain and honest patterns. Sobriety had become chic once again, and true refinement was to be sought in quietly elegant design.

A new epoch began with the introduction of weaving machinery and chemical dyes during the Meiji period, which began just a century ago. These inventions of the West threatened for a while to overwhelm the traditional textile crafts of Japan. An incontinent passion for Westernization swept the country, and it was only through a reassertion of basic Japanese good taste that these crafts managed to survive at all. Today, of course, their output is limited, and their products are far more expensive than those of the machine. Fortunately, however, these hand-woven and hand-dyed products still enjoy a fairly steady demand, and the techniques of creating them have not been lost.

Since 1950, twenty-one men and women have been designated as living national treasures for their devotion to the study and preservation of traditional Japanese weaving and dyeing techniques. It is sad to report that six of these respected craftsmen had laid aside their tools forever before this book was conceived. The least honor we can do them is to mention their names here. They were Sadakichi Matsubara, Eiichi Yamada, Kihachi Tabata, Tameji Ueda, Kosuke Komiya, and Toshijiro Inagaki—all masters of traditional dyeing techniques.

喜田川平朗

HEIRO KITAGAWA

Master of Antique Styles

Heiro Kitagawa represents the seventeenth generation of the house of Tawaraya, a weaving shop established in Kyoto in 1467. Of the thirty-one textile houses set up in Kyoto in that year, after a civil war had almost completely destroyed the city, only the Tawaraya survives today. Its history is a long and distinguished one, and Kitagawa upholds its traditions in nothing less than noble style.

Like many other Japanese craftsmen who have become outstanding in the field of decorative design, he began his career as a student of painting. Immediately after graduation from painting school, however, he set about studying the textile art under his father, Heihachi Kitagawa, and in 1927 succeeded him as master of the Tawaraya. One of his father's chief interests was the costume of the Noh drama, but his mastery of old-style weaving techniques had also brought him the assignment of repairing and reproducing the examples of ancient fabrics in the Shoso-in, the eighth-century treasure repository at Nara. Kitagawa participated in this work and thus learned the specialized techniques of weaving *yusoku orimono,* fabrics of Chinese origin which the Japanese of earlier periods had adapted in unique ways of their own. Among these were the *aya* (silk damask) and *nishiki* (silk brocade) which had been used for court costumes in the Nara and Heian periods. He also acquired the even older technique of producing the thin silk gauze called *ra,* which had first appeared in the Asuka period and had fallen into disuse after the eighth century.

It was the study and revival of these ancient techniques that enabled Kitagawa to create a new, elegant style of his own in the weaving of fine fabrics. His methods are imbued with tradition, but his creations are far from mere copies of antique textiles. His assistance in the repair and reproduction of the Shoso-in fabrics and his intensive research into the technical history of weaving are also noteworthy contributions to the textile art of Japan. He has twice been named as a living national treasure: in 1956 for his *ra* and in 1960 for his *yusoku orimono.*

✦

Page 49 shows a corner of Kitagawa's shop at Nishijin, with reels of silk thread waiting to be used on the loom. On pages 50–51 we see Kitagawa in his shop against an intricate background of looms, thread-reeling devices, and the like. In the right foreground an assistant prepares reels of thread from skeins of newly dyed silk. It is cold here in winter, and Kitagawa uses only one kerosene stove. Like the other craftsmen of Kyoto, he works in a Spartan atmosphere. The sample of his *ra* (silk gauze) on page 52, patterned with arabesques of peonies and ivy on a blue ground, exhibits his absolute mastery of color and design. The fabric is owned by the National Commission for the Protection of Cultural Properties. On page 53, in appropriate symbolism of Kitagawa's craft, appears a section of one of his looms, with four shuttles resting against a background of warp threads.

深見重助

JUSUKE FUKAMI

Weaver of Decorative Sashes

The famous house of Matsubaya in Kyoto has a history of more than three hundred years in the textile arts, and Jusuke Fukami represents the thirteenth generation of the family that founded it in the Edo period. From boyhood he was trained by his father in the weaving technique known as *karagumi,* a highly complicated process used for the production of decorative sashes in a variety of colors and intricate patterns. The technique was introduced from China during the Nara period, and *karagumi* sashes were much favored from that time on as sword belts to accompany the ceremonial costumes of noblemen and as decorative adjuncts to the vestments of priests.

Jusuke Fukami is the undisputed master of the *karagumi* technique. The layman, however, can only be baffled at its intricacy and the incredible amount of labor it requires. To begin with, the cord is all dyed by hand with vegetable dyes. "Of course," says Fukami, "I do the dyeing myself, but the important thing is the quality of the silk. The best silk comes from silkworms fed on the leaves of very old mulberry trees, and such silk is not easy to find nowadays." The dyeing alone may take a whole year, but the weaving is even more laborious, for some three hundred to four hundred separate cords are required to form the patterns in a single *karagumi* sash, and in a sash five centimeters wide, for example, the maximum length that can be woven in a day is no more than one centimeter. Small wonder, then, that the weaving of a single sash can take as much as two years. Small wonder, either, that Fukami's sashes are fabulously expensive, ranging from perhaps five hundred dollars to a thousand or more. In fact, because of their costliness they are used today only as accessories to ceremonial costumes like those, for example, of priests at the Grand Shrine of Ise.

Although he is now in his eighties, Fukami works faithfully at his craft. In 1956, his long devotion to traditional *karagumi* weaving brought him nomination as a living national treasure. In 1966, when the Kiwanis Club of Japan awarded him a cultural prize, he said: "If there is anything in my long life that deserves an award, it is not the work itself but the desire to preserve a tradition." It is sad indeed to think that Fukami will have no successor, for he is the last of his line.

✦

On page 55 appear two sections of a Fukami *karagumi* sash owned by the National Commission for the Protection of Cultural Properties. Even the briefest glance reveals the astonishing exquisiteness of the weaving. The colors, all produced by natural dyes, are no less exquisite than the weaving itself. On pages 56–57, Fukami demonstrates the extreme complexity of the *karagumi* technique. The arrangement of the bobbins for this complicated style of weaving (pages 58–59) requires tremendous patience and care, but Fukami is not to be hurried. Pride of craftsmanship is everything, and time is not his master but his servant.

木村雨山

UZAN KIMURA

Dyer of Kaga Yuzen

Perhaps Japan's greatest invention in the art of dyeing is the technique of *yuzen*, the intricate paste-resist process used to produce the exquisite effects seen in the formal kimono of countless Japanese women: floral and bird designs and other motifs from nature in superb color and elegance of line. The invention of the process is attributed to the Edo-period artist whose name it bears, Miyazaki Yuzen, and its birthplace was Kaga Province (now Ishikawa Prefecture). In time, Kaga *yuzen* came to be distinguished from that produced in other areas, and such variations as Kyoto and Edo *yuzen* appeared.

Uzan Kimura was born in the milieu of Kaga *yuzen*. He was, in effect, a man of art from the beginning. As student, craftsman, and teacher, he has devoted his life to the preservation and enhancement of traditional techniques. His singularly creative imagination has brought a decidedly modern freshness to Kaga *yuzen* dyeing, and it was for this achievement that he was named a living national treasure in 1955.

Since the designs for Kaga *yuzen* are drawn on the fabric without stencils, and since the paste resist (to retain the outlines of color areas and to reserve one color against another) must be applied with extreme delicacy, and again without stencils, the process demands consummate skill and precision. Here Kimura has no equal, and his employment of rich colors makes his patterns glow with life.

Of his work, Kimura says, with typical modesty: "Both my materials and my ideas come from nature and everyday life. Sometimes I draw pine trees, sometimes peonies. I never deliberately search for design ideas. They often come to me by chance when I wake up in the morning. In fact, I get some of my best ideas while I'm still in bed. The morning hours are the most important, and unless I work hard in the morning I feel rather lazy all day."

✦

In the facing photograph, Kimura applies the finishing touches of color to a brilliant design of roses on a fabric intended for a young woman's kimono. The sample of floral-patterned Kaga *yuzen* on page 62 (here folded to give the effect of a made-up kimono) displays the distinctly modern touch that marks Kimura's adaptation of traditional techniques and designs. On page 63, against the background of the reed floor mat on which he often works, we see several symbols of his craft: the sharply pointed brushes and the dishes for the indigo juice in which he traces the basic patterns over which the paste resist will be applied. (Both indigo and paste will be washed out when the dyeing is completed.) On page 64 Kimura applies paste resist to a complicated floral design. The photograph on page 65 shows him in a characteristic working position: sprawled on the floor, with a low folding screen to keep off drafts and dust. Here he is using indigo juice to trace a design on a kimono.

中村勝馬

KATSUMA NAKAMURA

Dyer of Edo Yuzen

Katsuma Nakamura is not by any means a traditionalist, even though his specialty is *yuzen* dyeing in Edo style—that is, the style of Tokyo in the feudal days when the city was still called Edo. His introduction of new designs and colors, often considered quite daring by craftsmen who adhere more closely to *yuzen* traditions, distinctly marks him as an innovator. Nor has he hesitated to introduce new techniques. And yet, for all of this, his work reflects the long-standing ideals of *yuzen* craftsmanship.

As early as 1913 he was startling (and attracting) people with such extremely "modern" designs as his "poplars and birds of passage," which adorned the skirt of a woman's ceremonial kimono and won him a prize. It was not the theme so much as the treatment that was exciting, and before long he was recognized as a master of *yuzen* in the modern style. In 1929 the famous Mitsukoshi Department Store in Tokyo employed him as a designer, and there, one after another, he introduced brilliant new ideas in Edo *yuzen.*

His interest in new techniques also brought fresh blood into *yuzen* dyeing. He discovered, for example, that interesting and modern effects could be obtained by stippling the fabric with paste resist instead of using the traditional paper tube to apply it. Such a method was completely unknown in the annals of *yuzen,* and the use of it added to Nakamura's reputation as a creator of new and dynamic patterns. His talent for breathing life into the dyeing of Edo *yuzen* won him recognition as a living national treasure in 1955.

Nakamura insists that *yuzen* dyeing must not be considered merely a part of the making of a kimono. "The emphasis," he says, "must be on producing a piece of beautifully dyed material which can be used to make a kimono, not on the finished garment itself. In a word, the important thing is not the kimono but the creation of excellent design."

✦

On the facing page appear part of a preliminary sketch for one of Nakamura's designs, a charcoal sketching pencil, and a feather brush used for keeping the sketch clean. Pages 68–69 show him at work on the sketch of the preceding photograph: a design for a man's *hakama* or full skirtlike trousers for ceremonial wear. The following two pages (70–71) reproduce a section of a Nakamura *susomoyo* or woman's formal kimono whose decoration is limited to the bottom of the skirt. The design here is a favorite Japanese motif: *Korin-nami* (Korin waves)—that is, waves in the style of the celebrated Edo-period artist Ogata Korin. Of particular interest is the exquisite fine-line dyeing, to which touches of gold embroidery have been added to create a sumptuous effect. (The kimono is owned by the National Commission for the Protection of Cultural Properties.) Pages 72–73 illustrate the Nakamura technique of applying paste resist by stippling.

白
青

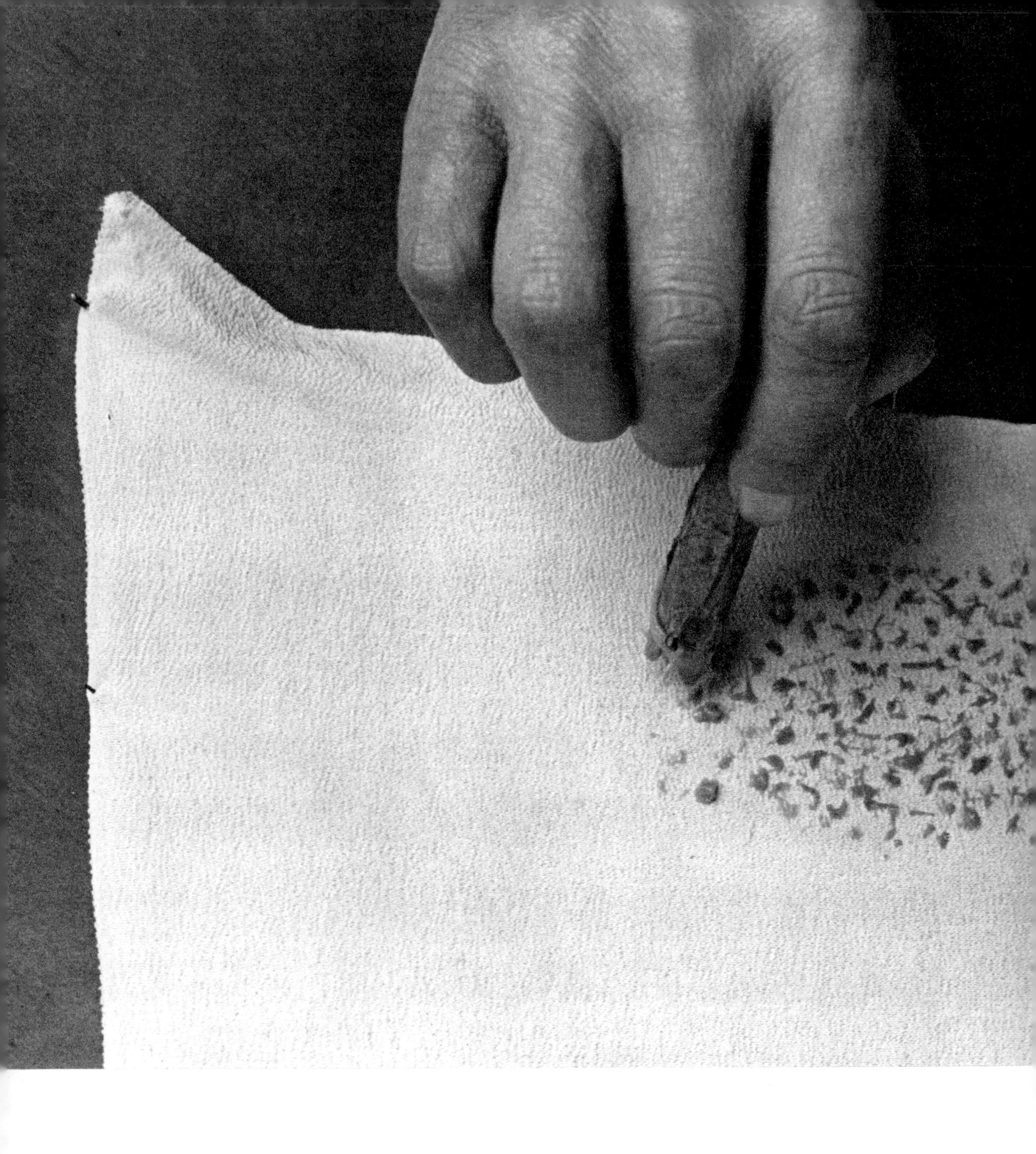

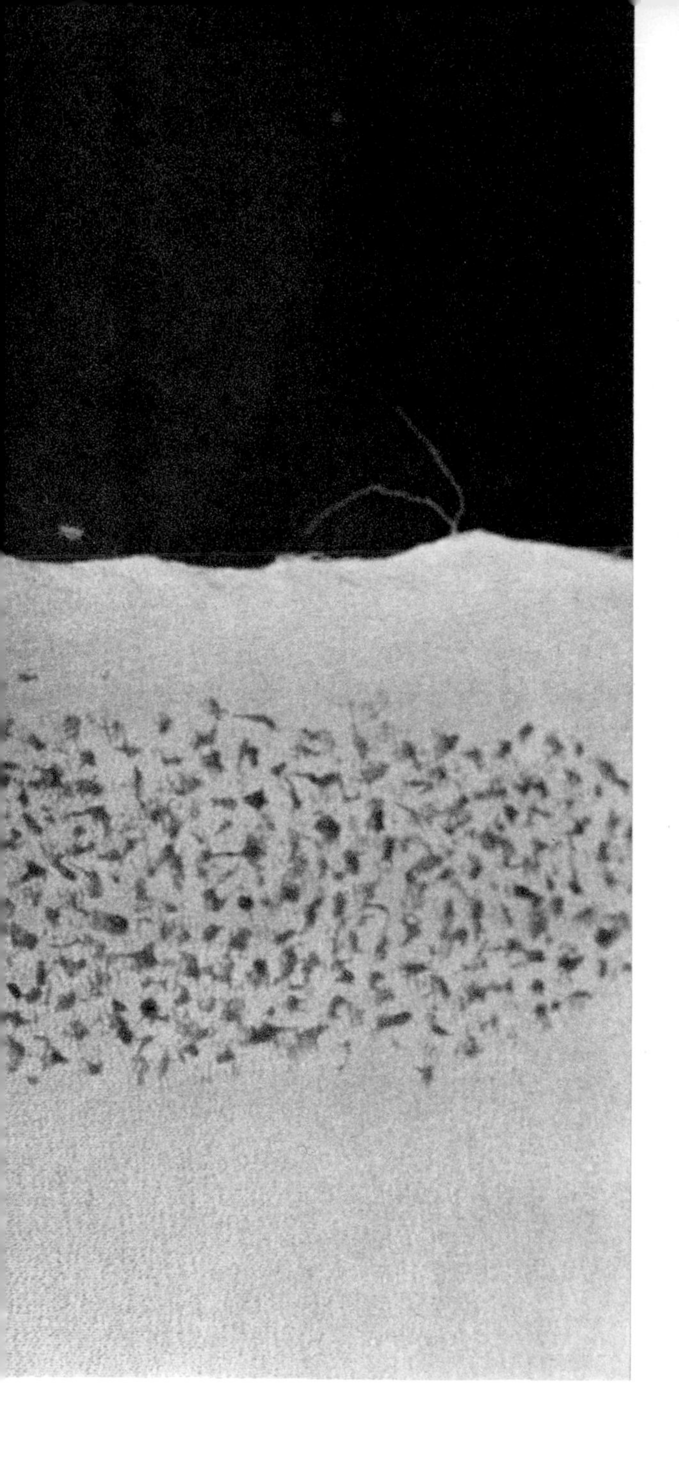

芹沢銈介

KEISUKE SERIZAWA

Master of Stencil Dyeing

Like the potter Shoji Hamada (pages 24–34), Keisuke Serizawa is essentially a folk artist, and his contributions to the traditional art of stencil dyeing are as significant as those of Hamada to the art of folk pottery. Again like Hamada, he is a leader in the folk-art movement initiated by Soetsu Yanagi some fifty years ago.

As a student of design and traditional handicrafts, Serizawa was particularly impressed by two textile-dyeing techniques: the *bingata* of the Ryukyu Islands and the Ise *katagami* of Mie Prefecture (pages 90–106), both of which were used to produce stencil-dyed fabrics of venerable ancestry and charmingly unsophisticated design. It was from such inspirations that he derived his own *kataezome,* the stencil dyeing for which he has become celebrated among modern Japanese designers and dyers. For this achievement he was named a living national treasure in 1956.

Serizawa's style is never mistaken for that of other artists in the field. His design is vigorous and forthright, and his resolute colors have a distinctly rural touch. It would be wrong, however, to speak of this as naïveté, for there is a certain sophistication about Serizawa's style that sets him apart from the anonymous folk artists whose traditions he upholds. Nor has he confined his work to textiles alone. His stencil-dyed papers are as well known as his fabrics, and they are put to a multiplicity of uses: for sliding doors and decorative screens, for book covers, for the striking calendars that he produces every year—to mention but a few.

In spite of having reached his seventies, Serizawa gives an engaging impression of youthfulness, and this is reflected in his designs. The many assistants in his studio are proud of working for him, and they find in him not a stern taskmaster but a warmhearted gentleman. Always alert to new ideas, he nevertheless holds firm to the basic traditions of his art.

✦

In the facing photograph, Serizawa is seen at the entrance of one of the several workshops that make up his studio in Tokyo. Here he inspects a length of stencil-dyed cloth which is being stretched and dried. On the following pages (76–77) he enjoys a moment of relaxation in the workshop where his fabrics are made up into such items as place mats and *noren,* the divided curtains traditionally hung in the doorways of shops, restaurants, teahouses, and the like. Pages 78–79 display one of Serizawa's masterworks: a six-panel screen mounted with stencil-dyed cloth in a design embodying the symbols of the Japanese *hiragana* syllabary and various motifs of traditional decoration in folk-art style. This screen, owned by the National Commission for the Protection of Cultural Properties, expresses the essence of Serizawa's vigorous and masculine style.

いろはにほへとち

りぬるをわかよた

れそつねならむう

清水幸太郎

KOTARO SHIMIZU

Dyer of Nagaita Chugata

Nagaita chugata (literally, "long board, medium-size pattern") is a type of stencil dyeing in which whole bolts of cloth are stretched on a table some six meters long and stenciled with a repeat pattern that is neither large and bold nor small enough to be called minute. Like *yuzen* dyeing, it makes use of a paste resist, but the colors are limited to blue and white. This is one of the traditional methods of dyeing cloth for the *yukata,* the unlined cotton kimono favored for summer wear. The technique, which has been practiced since the Edo period, is a laborious one, for it requires not only the cutting of intricate stencils but also the greatest of care in applying the paste resist to avoid any indication of the places where the repeat stencil has been lifted and moved to the next section of cloth.

Kotaro Shimizu has been occupied at this exacting craft since childhood, when his father taught him the technique. As the successor to the family business of dyeing, he has adhered firmly to tradition, and his achievements were properly recognized when he was named a living national treasure in 1955. Although the technique itself permits a wide range of inventiveness in design, the *yukata* patterned with traditional motifs has always been preferred, and Shimizu is by no means unhappy that this should be so. He notes with a good deal of wryness, however, that people no longer prize fine *yukata* as they once did, since the machine has largely taken over from traditional craftsmen. "Machine-dyed *yukata* cloth is neither elegant nor color-fast," he says, "and nowadays the *yukata* itself is discarded after one summer's wear." At times he regrets, too, that neither of his two sons will succeed him in his craft. In fact, there is no successor in sight.

✦

The facing photograph shows Shimizu using a stencil to apply paste resist for a repeating design of folding fans and ripples in a stream. *Yukata* cloth is sold in bolts of standard length and width, one bolt serving to make a single garment. The section of Shimizu's workshop seen on pages 82–83 is symbolic of the plain and unaffected spirit in which he follows his craft. In fact, except for one or two items like the modern-style spectacles, this might be a workshop of Edo times. A stencil-cutting board appears in the lower half of the picture. Page 84 shows a detail of the fan-and-ripple-patterned fabric of page 81. The detail of a *yukata* shown on page 85 illustrates the astonishing delicacy of Shimizu's work at its finest. The design of decorated clam shells against a background simulating a gauze weave is done entirely by means of a stencil. Here it appears in considerably reduced size (the clam shells are actually about the size of a fist), but the intricacy of the stencil can be appreciated nonetheless. The seam represents the joining of two sections of the fabric at the back of the *yukata.*

森口華弘

KAKO MORIGUCHI

Dyer of Yuzen Makinori

Kako Moriguchi was named as a living national treasure in 1967 for his remarkable inventiveness in *yuzen makinori,* a traditional type of *yuzen* dyeing done by the "sown paste" *(makinori)* method. In this technique, dried paste resist in granulated form is "sown" on wet fabric to form the pattern, and the dyes are applied with brushes to produce effects similar to those of pointillism in painting. The technique originated in the Edo period, but it remained for Moriguchi to revive it in newly creative fashion.

Just as Uzan Kimura (pages 60–65) is identified with Kaga *yuzen* and Katsuma Nakamura (pages 66–73) with *yuzen* in Edo style, so Moriguchi may be said to represent the *yuzen* of Kyoto. His style, however, sets him apart from most other Kyoto dyeing artists, for he gives first place to the creation of new and strikingly fresh designs instead of following traditional patterns. His themes are from nature and Japanese life, but he stylizes them in a decorative manner that is peculiarly his own.

Like many other Japanese masters of textile design, Moriguchi combined the study of painting with that of dyeing techniques. As a young man, he became fascinated with the beauty of Kyoto *yuzen* fabrics. He knew quite early what his craft was to be, and he set about to master its traditional techniques. Traditional designs, however, were another matter, and he saw no chance for true creativity in merely following them. "Loyalty to tradition does not mean remaining static," Moriguchi says. "After all, those who originated the traditions were creative, and those who follow them must be creative too. My methods are old, but I want my designs to be new. The honest creations of today will be part of tomorrow's tradition."

✦

On the facing page, Moriguchi sets to work on a new *yuzen makinori* design. The granulated paste resist is made by first grinding dried *mochi* (rice which has been steamed and pounded to a gluey consistency) into powder, next mixing it with water to form a kind of glue, and then drying it again on sections of bamboo sheath. The wet fabric is stretched tightly before being "sown" with the paste resist. After paste and fabric have dried, the dyeing begins. The effects produced in the dyeing are seen on page 88, which shows a detail of Moriguchi's decorative screen called "Sea of Clouds." It requires hardly more than a glance to reveal the infinite concentration that the *makinori* technique calls for—to say nothing of the inventiveness with which Moriguchi employs it. The brushes he uses for applying his dyes (page 89) are fitting symbols of his astonishing craftsmanship.

88

伊勢型紙

SIX MASTERS OF THE PAPER STENCIL

The paper dyeing stencils known as Ise *katagami* are named after the Ise region in Mie Prefecture, where they have been made since the early Edo period. Today their manufacture centers in the town of Suzuka in that region, and some eighty craftsmen are engaged in producing them. Of these masters of Ise *katagami,* no fewer than six have been named as living national treasures, an honor conferred on them in 1955.

The stencils, still made by traditional techniques, are used by dyers throughout Japan and have thus played an important role in the textile arts. Although they serve mainly for the dyeing of kimono fabrics, they are also used in the production of decorative papers for sliding doors, screens, and the like. The preponderance of machine-made stencils and machine-dyed textiles in the present age has greatly reduced the popularity of the Ise *katagami,* but the craftsmen of Suzuka have not surrendered their integrity, for they know that no machine can match the skill of the human hand in producing imaginative designs.

The Ise stencils are cut from strong handmade paper, several sheets of which are pasted together with persimmon tannin to give greater strength and durability. Usually a number of stencils are cut simultaneously, and since some of the more complicated designs require as many as nine hundred openings in a space only about 3.3 centimeters square, only the most skilled of craftsmen can accomplish the work with the necessary exactness. And even when as many as twelve stencils are cut at the same time, all are exactly alike.

Of the six living national treasures among the makers of Ise stencils, Yoshimatsu Nambu is outstanding for his *tsukibori,* a method of cutting with a thin, needle-pointed knife. On page 92 he is seen at work on a graceful floral pattern for dyeing kimono fabric. Here, with a precision that is hardly less than magical, he is cutting twelve stencils at the same time. The beauty of his designs—to say nothing of their intricacy—is displayed in the section of a stencil shown on page 93. Nambu has followed his craft since boyhood, when he first learned the techniques from a stern master who, he insists, did not teach him but forced him to learn by himself.

Yujiro Nakamura is a master of the technique of *dogubori,* which employs a variety of punchlike knives to create the small patterns known as *komon.* On pages 94–95 he is occupied with one of his typical designs. Since he pushes the knife with his right cheek, he has developed a callus there, but it would be wrong to regard this as a disfigurement, for it is an honorable mark of his craft. His knives (page 96) are all made by hand. "When you make the tools yourself," says Nakamura, "they will move the way you want them to." Although his stencils display a rather quiet simplicity, they are anything but simple to make, and the multiplicity of tools that he keeps in a corner of his workshop (page 97) attests to the intricacy of his work.

Baiken Rokutani, master of *kiribori,* has achieved distinction with his incredibly minute work in geometric designs, for which he employs an augerlike knife with a tiny blade in half-moon shape. Like Nakamura, he makes his own tools, and he uses them with fascinating precision to produce such remarkable stencils as the eight which he is cutting simultaneously on page 98. The detail of this work on page 99 reveals the great subtlety of his designs.

The *shimabori* technique of Hiroshi Kodama is perhaps the most difficult of all stencilmaking techniques, for it requires the cutting of infinitely fine lines to create stripes of various delicate patterns. Kodama devotes himself to this technique alone, and he has mastered it completely. The photograph on page 100 reveals the strict precision with which he works, drawing the knife toward him to cut the lines. Later, fine threads will be pasted over the stencil to strengthen it. The almost unbelievable intricacy of Kodama's work can be seen in the stencil shown on page 101.

Like Yujiro Nakamura (pages 94–97), Hidekichi Nakajima is a maker of *dogubori* stencils. His workshop (pages 102–3) is typical of those of the Suzuka stencilmakers, and it speaks of his devotion to his craft. There is an antique flavor about it in spite of the presence of such modern appurtenances as the electric light and the radio. The charcoal brazier at lower right supplies his only heat in winter, and he uses the electric light both night and day to assure perfection in his work. Even at eighty-four, he continues at his craft with energy and interest, and both he and his workshop seem somehow to express the essence of traditional craftsmanship.*

As the last of the living national treasures in this group, Mie Jonokuchi has been honored for her superb ability in the important work of strengthening delicate stencils by pasting fine silk thread over them. The reel of thread suspended from the ceiling of her workshop (page 104) is symbolic of her craft. On pages 105–6 she demonstrates her technique, first drawing lengths of thread from the reel (upper left), next tying them to the numerous nails on a special frame (lower left), then placing the stencil on the frame (upper right) and brushing it with persimmon tannin (lower right), and finally (page 106) blowing the threads to make them adhere to the stencil. This last step is particularly important, for the threads must not be so tight that they warp the stencil when they dry.

✦

NOTE. See the stencil reproduced on the endpapers of this book for an example of *shimabori* and thread-strengthening techniques similar to those used by Hiroshi Kodama and Mie Jonokuchi.

* Hidekichi Nakajima died on February 2, 1968, at the age of eighty-four, only a few days before this book went to press.

南部芳松

YOSHIMATSU NAMBU

中村勇二郎

YUJIRO NAKAMURA

SOLE
十二
十一
五

六谷梅軒

BAIKEN ROKUTANI

児玉 博 HIROSHI KODAMA

中島秀吉

HIDEKICHI NAKAJIMA

城之口みえ

MIE JONOKUCHI

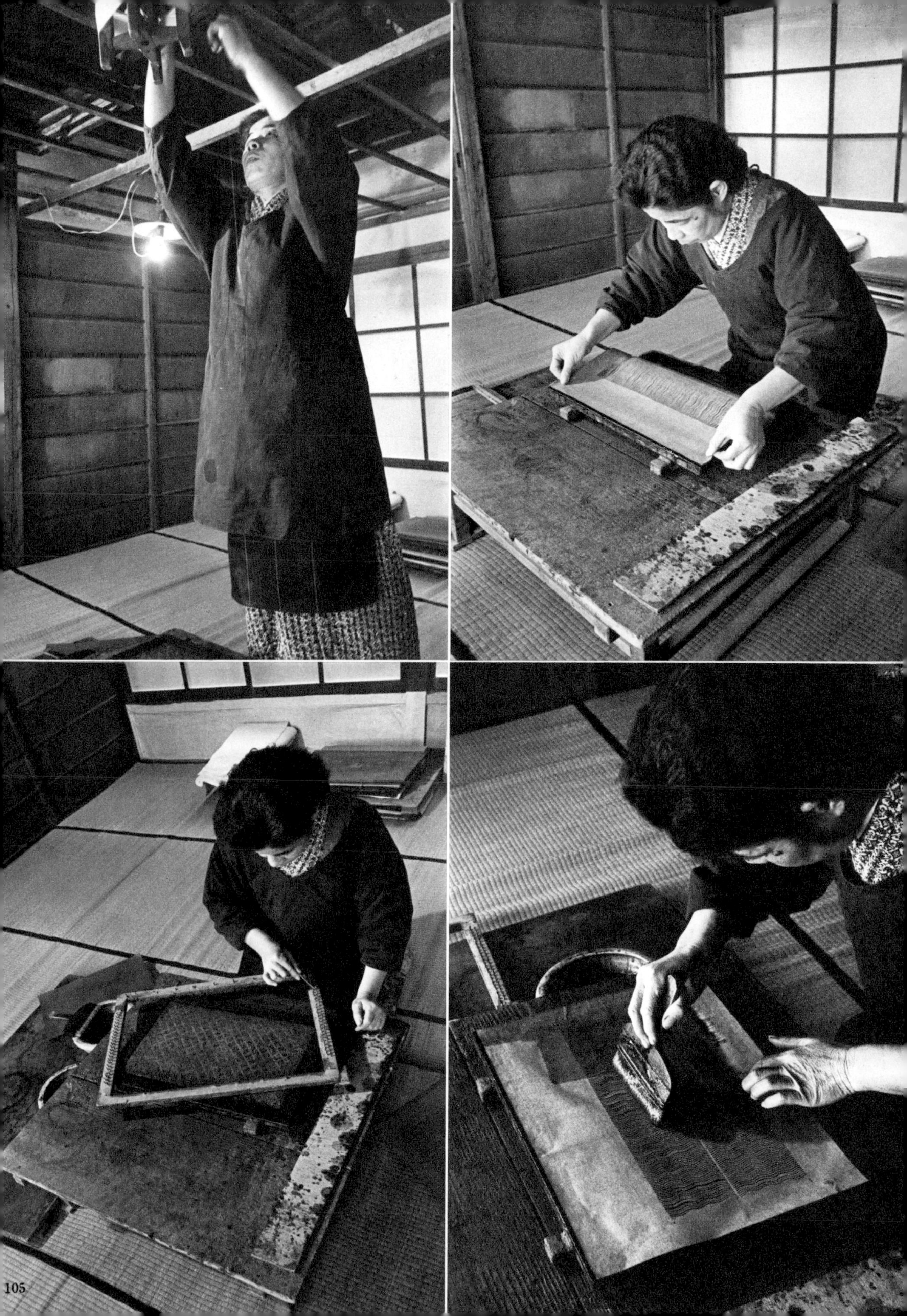

千葉あやの

AYANO CHIBA

Indigo Dyer and Weaver

Ayano Chiba, of the town of Kurikoma in Miyagi Prefecture, is probably the last of Japanese textile craftsmen to use the method of indigo dyeing known as *shoaizome*. She is remarkable not only for preserving a traditional and charmingly naïve technique but also for performing every step of the process herself, from growing and drying the indigo and spinning the raw flax into thread to weaving the cloth and dyeing it. She is a true primitive among Japanese craftsmen and a strict upholder of tradition. It was for her *shoaizome* that she was named a living national treasure in 1955.

Ayano Chiba's home is in the remote countryside of the Tohoku region, a three-hour drive from the city of Sendai, and she speaks the authentic dialect of the region—a dialect so broad, in fact, that it is almost unintelligible to a Japanese from Tokyo. She was born in this region, has grown old there, and has maintained the technique that sets the indigo dyeing of Tohoku apart from that of all other regions of the country.

Her method of preparing the dye differs from the much more generally used method of boiling the indigo first and then allowing it to ferment. She uses the heat of the summer sun to produce natural fermentation, and a cold mountain river that runs by her house supplies the water that is most important to her craft. Even among traditional craftsmen, few live so close to nature as Ayano Chiba does, and nature pervades her work.

Certainly her craft is a humble one, and it is by no means a fruitful source of income. In fact, she lives the plainest of lives. And yet, watching her go about her laborious work, the viewer feels humble too, for he knows that she gives it the utmost in affection.

✦

Ayano Chiba (facing page), for all her seventy-eight years, retains an alert and unflagging interest in her work. On pages 110–11 we see her on the veranda of her house, where an elderly assistant helps her strip off the dried indigo leaves from which she makes her dye. The state of the sliding doors, crudely repaired with pages from magazines, advertising posters, and other odds and ends of paper, shows clearly that her household is far from affluent. Outside the entrance to the house (page 112) she demonstrates another step in the preparation of the dye: crushing the dried indigo leaves on a straw mat. Her loom (page 113) is no less primitive and traditional than the other accessories of her craft. On page 114 she inspects lengths of cloth which have just been lifted from the dye vat. The vat on page 115 was presented to her by the town mayor in honor of her designation as a living national treasure.

寝具まつり

NALBRON

甲田栄佑

EISUKE KODA

Master of the "Exquisite Sendai Weave"

Eisuke Koda is the master of a weaving technique that was once decreed a trade secret by the feudal lords of the Sendai area in northern Japan. The technique, known as the "exquisite Sendai weave," originated in Kyoto and was brought to the city of Sendai around the middle of the Edo period. There it was employed in the weaving of fabrics for *hakama,* the full skirtlike trousers worn by men as part of traditional ceremonial costume. Since the feudal lords and high-ranking officials of the Sendai region monopolized the output of the weavers who produced these fine *hakama* fabrics, they prohibited outsiders from learning the technique, and the craft of the "exquisite Sendai weave" remained a purely local one.

Today, of course, the feudal rulers of Sendai have long since vanished from the scene, and the superb weaving technique that once produced their *hakama* has almost vanished with them. In fact, Eisuke Koda is thought to be the only weaver who still practices it in traditional style. His chief patrons are Noh actors and classical-style dancers—men who themselves uphold venerable traditions and insist on the finest of fabrics for their costumes.

The "exquisite Sendai weave" is done in pure silk, and one of the remarkable features of the technique is that the warp threads must be wet during the weaving, so that the finished *hakama* will be extremely durable but not inordinately stiff. Interestingly enough, *hakama* made of Koda's fabrics are said to be able to stand up by themselves and yet never to become wrinkled when the wearer sits down. Koda's production is necessarily small—from five to ten *hakama* lengths a month—for he uses only a single hand loom and does all the weaving himself.

Koda represents the third generation in the family trade of weaving *hakama* fabrics. He learned his craft from his father and the well-known master Manjiro Sayama and has followed it since the early years of this century. Patience and tenacity have long been characteristic of people in northern Japan, and Koda displays these virtues to perfection in his exacting work. He was named a living national treasure in 1956.

✦

Dyeing the thread (page 117) is the first step in the weaving of Koda's fabrics, and this, like everything else—including selection of the raw silk and the dyes—he does himself. Here he uses sections of bamboo to wring out skeins of thread after the dye bath. In his unpretentious workshop (pages 118–19) stands the hundred-year-old hand loom on which he produces his " exquisite Sendai weave." Page 120 shows a section of one of his fabrics on the loom together with two fitting symbols of his craft: a shuttle and two reels of silk thread.

THE ART OF THE LACQUER CRAFTSMAN

If Japan is celebrated as a country of ceramics, it is hardly less celebrated as a country of lacquer. In fact, in Victorian days the name of Japan itself became a synonym for the products of Japanese lacquer craftsmen that found their way to England and America, and one spoke of buying such things as japan boxes and japan trays. Not in England and America alone, of course, but in other countries as well, the lacquer ware of Japan excited intense admiration, and it is hardly a cause for wonder that the name of the country should have become a name for one of its famous products, just as the word "china" once meant fine porcelain.

It must be pointed out, however, that the craft of lacquer is not exclusively Japanese. It was known in Egypt as early as 3000 B.C. and in China at least as early as the time of Emperor Shih Huang Ti (third century B.C.), from whose tomb a number of lacquer-decorated objects have been recovered. The techniques of lacquer were also known in India and the countries of Southeast Asia, and there is no doubt that influences from the Middle East as well as from the Asian continent had their effect on Japanese lacquer art. In ancient times such influences penetrated very slowly, and they reached Japan by way of China and Korea. Although it is true, then, that Japan cannot claim invention of the craft, it is also true that Japanese artists brought it to perfection.

There are a number of reasons for this achievement, but the principal one is that Japanese culture made great use of wood, not only for architecture but also for sculpture and for innumerable objects of everyday use, including such various items as saddles, footgear, and tableware. And wood, of course, is the base most commonly used for lacquer ware. The lacquer itself originally served the purpose of making wood moistureproof and more durable, but its decorative possibilities were quickly discovered. Ways of varying its color were invented, and numerous techniques for embellishing it with other materials appeared. Lacquer techniques were constantly refined, and lacquer ware became an intimate part of daily life in Japan.

Archaeological research has revealed that the use of lacquer in Japan dates back to the Stone Age. In those remote days, however, it was not used for the production of handicraft objects but for adhesive purposes such as strengthening and fastening ropes made of vine. During the prehistoric Jomon and Yayoi periods (roughly from 4000 B.C. to A.D. 250) earthenware was painted with lacquer, sometimes in various colors, sometimes with designs, both to increase its durability and to add decorative interest. But here lacquer was merely an adjunct to the craft of ceramics, and it is not until much later in history that we have any surviving examples of lacquer as a handicraft in itself.

The seventh-century Tamamushi Shrine, a miniature construction preserved at the Horyu-ji, in Nara, and the numerous pieces of lacquer ware among the eighth-century treasures of the Shoso-in (also in Nara) are the earliest works in which we can see the art of Japanese lacquer craftsmen displayed in its own right. The Tamamushi Shrine and its lower base are painted with plain lacquer, and its four sides, as well as the panels of its square pedestal, are ornamented with Buddhist paintings in various colors of lacquer on a black lacquer ground. The Shoso-in pieces include a large number of boxes in which lacquer covers a base of wood, bamboo, leather, or cloth, as well as musical instruments whose lacquer surface is splendidly decorated with designs in gold, silver, and mother-of-pearl.

At least as far back as the seventh and eighth centuries, then, and particularly during the Nara period (710–94), Japanese craftsmen were experimenting with new techniques of lacquer decoration. From Nara times date such traditional methods as those of embedding extremely thin pieces of gold and silver (the *heidatsu* method) or mother-of-pearl (the *raden* method) in the wet lacquer surface to create a design, adding another coat of lacquer, and then polishing the surface to a brilliant luster. A more important technique of the Nara-period craftsmen, however, was that of *maki-e* (literally, "sown picture"), in which gold or silver dust was "sown" on the wet lacquer surface to form the design. In some cases no further lacquering was done, but in others the surface was relacquered and polished to give more brilliance to the ornamentation. *Maki-e* was once thought to be a purely Japanese invention, but recent research has shown that it existed in ancient China, long before the Nara period began. It is not known, though, whether the Nara craftsmen developed the technique on their own or whether they borrowed it from their Chinese predecessors.

The techniques of Nara times were further refined during the succeeding Heian period (794–1185), and there exist from this period several masterpieces in *maki-e,* including a Chinese-style chest decorated with a design of plovers and water plants (in the Kongobu-ji on Mount Koya) and a cosmetic box with a design of cart wheels in a stream (owned by the National Commission for the Protection of Cultural Properties). Mother-of-pearl was often used to accent the *maki-e* design, as in the case of the cosmetic box just mentioned.

During the Kamakura period (late twelfth to early fourteenth century) the *maki-e* technique became more elaborate, and such variations as *takamaki-e* (*maki-e* designs in relief) were created. This period also saw the introduction of a new technique in which layers of different-colored lacquer were applied and then carved to make a design in one color appear against a background of another.

The lacquer art of the Muromachi and Momoyama periods (late fourteenth to seventeenth century) continued to place emphasis on *maki-e*. The influence of Ming lacquer ware was particularly strong in Muromachi times, and designs were often copied from Chinese paintings. Momoyama lacquer, on the other hand, tended to emphasize purely decorative rather than pictorial design, and influences from the West inspired a greater use of color. An important Momoyama development was the revival of painted design in lacquer decoration—a technique once popular in the Asuka and Nara periods.

The lacquer art of the Edo period (seventeenth to mid-nineteenth century) attained its highest level in the work of Hon'ami Koetsu and Ogata Korin, two masters of the decorative style. Koetsu revived the elegant designs of the Heian period, infusing them with new vigor and a daring creativeness that seems modern even today. He also developed a *maki-e* technique of his own to produce ornamentation in simple but lively style. Korin, in his lacquer pieces, expressed the same decorative boldness and subtle stylization that characterize his superbly painted screens. After Koetsu and Korin, however, techniques and designs became ever more elaborate and complicated. A certain formality set in, and the artistic level was lowered.

Nevertheless, in certain provincial areas where feudal lords encouraged the craft of lacquer—just as they encouraged the crafts of ceramics and weaving—a number of traditional local wares of considerable artistry were produced. These, of course, were much closer to the life of the common people than the oversophisticated creations of stylish urban craftsmen, and they expressed the vigor and wholesomeness of genuine folkcraft products. Among such regional wares were those of Tsugaru and Aizu in northern Honshu, Wajima and Wakasa in Ishikawa Prefecture, and the Shunkei lacquer produced at Sakai, near Osaka.

It was the arrival of Japan's modern period, just a century ago, that brought Japanese lacquer ware to its position of renown in the West. Ironically, however, this same event marked the beginning of a disastrous decline in the craft itself, which could not compete with the machine in turning out large quantities of relatively inexpensive products like those which have more and more replaced the traditional lacquer ware of the past. It is a regrettable fact that the craft is most inactive in present-day Japan and in many ways has the aspect of a dying art.

The four living national treasures who represent the craft of lacquer are among the very few who continue to produce wares of quality today. One can readily see why such high value is placed upon the work of these four outstanding men. Their determination to uphold a cherished tradition merits nothing less than the honor that has been conferred upon them.

Two of these artists, Gonroku Matsuda and Shozan Takano, are famous for their skill in the *maki-e* technique. We have already noted the prominent role played by this technique in the history of Japanese lacquer art. Matsuda and Takano have not only preserved its traditions but have also found ways to give it new life in the modern age. It is not easy, however, to sustain a tradition in the face of overwhelming industrialization and a constantly lessening demand for handicraft products that were once in almost universal use.

Kodo Otomaru has mastered the complex technique of *choshitsu,* in which designs are produced by carving through layers of different-colored lacquer or by filling a carved design in a monochrome surface with other colors. He works in the tradition of the Edo-period craftsman Zokoku, who is celebrated for his *choshitsu* lacquer.

Taiho Mae springs from a regional tradition: that of the Wajima lacquer craftsmen of Ishikawa Prefecture. He is an expert in the *chinkin* technique, in which patterns carved in the lacquer surface are filled with gold foil. Although he is essentially a follower of the traditional Wajima techniques, he has infused them with fresh blood, and his work has a distinctly modern air.

It must be reported with deep regret that another lacquer artist of distinction is no longer among the living national treasures. He was Joshin Isoi, and he was honored for his splendid work in the traditional technique of color inlay known as *kimma.*

松田權六

GONROKU MATSUDA

Classicist in Maki-e

The city of Kanazawa, in Ishikawa Prefecture, was once the seat of the powerful clan of Maeda, feudal lords of Kaga, as the region was then called. During the Edo period it was the policy of the clan to encourage the handicraft industries of Kaga to greater development, and Kanazawa became noted as a production center for ceramics, dyed textiles (for example, the Kaga *yuzen* described earlier in this book), and lacquer. Among these products the lacquer ware was outstanding, and the lacquer craftsmen of Kanazawa established a national reputation for their excellent work.

It was in this city that Gonroku Matsuda was born. His family owned a lacquer workshop, and he was initiated into the craft at the age of seven. From then on, there was no doubt concerning what his career was to be, but his special admiration for the *maki-e* technique led him to become its modern master. As we have noted, this method of decorating a wet lacquer surface with powdered or finely cut gold (or sometimes silver or even tin) originated some twelve centuries ago in the Nara period and is the most prominent of traditional lacquer techniques. Matsuda's contribution to the art of *maki-e* is represented in the remarkable delicacy and elegance of his style, which clearly marks him as a classicist. Behind the evolution of this style are years of painstaking study and research, and it is important to note that the research goes on, even though the style may seem to have been perfected long since. In 1955 he was honored for his achievements in *maki-e* by being named a living national treasure.

Matsuda lives and works in the frenetic environment of Tokyo, but in his workshop he has created a tranquil world of his own. His work itself, his continuing research, and his numerous activities in the promotion of the handicraft arts make him anything but a man of leisure. In his workshop, however, he refuses to be hurried. "If you worry about the time," he says, "you will never produce a decent piece of lacquer."

✦

In the facing photograph, Matsuda draws a basic pattern of pine branches on a stationery box. The design will emerge in brilliant gold when the surface is given a final polishing. The following two pages (128–29) picture an array of his tools, including bamboo tubes and brushes for applying the gold dust, styluses for drawing fine lines in the lacquer, and other implements for creating special effects. His workshop, a corner of which appears on page 130, is immaculate, for dust is the enemy of lacquer, and the windows here are provided with triple sliding panels to keep it out. The box on which he is working is typical of his modern-style *maki-e* creations. On page 131 is a Matsuda masterpiece: a traditional-style stationery box patterned in gold with a stylized bamboo grove and accented with delightfully drawn birds. It is owned by the National Commission for the Protection of Cultural Properties.

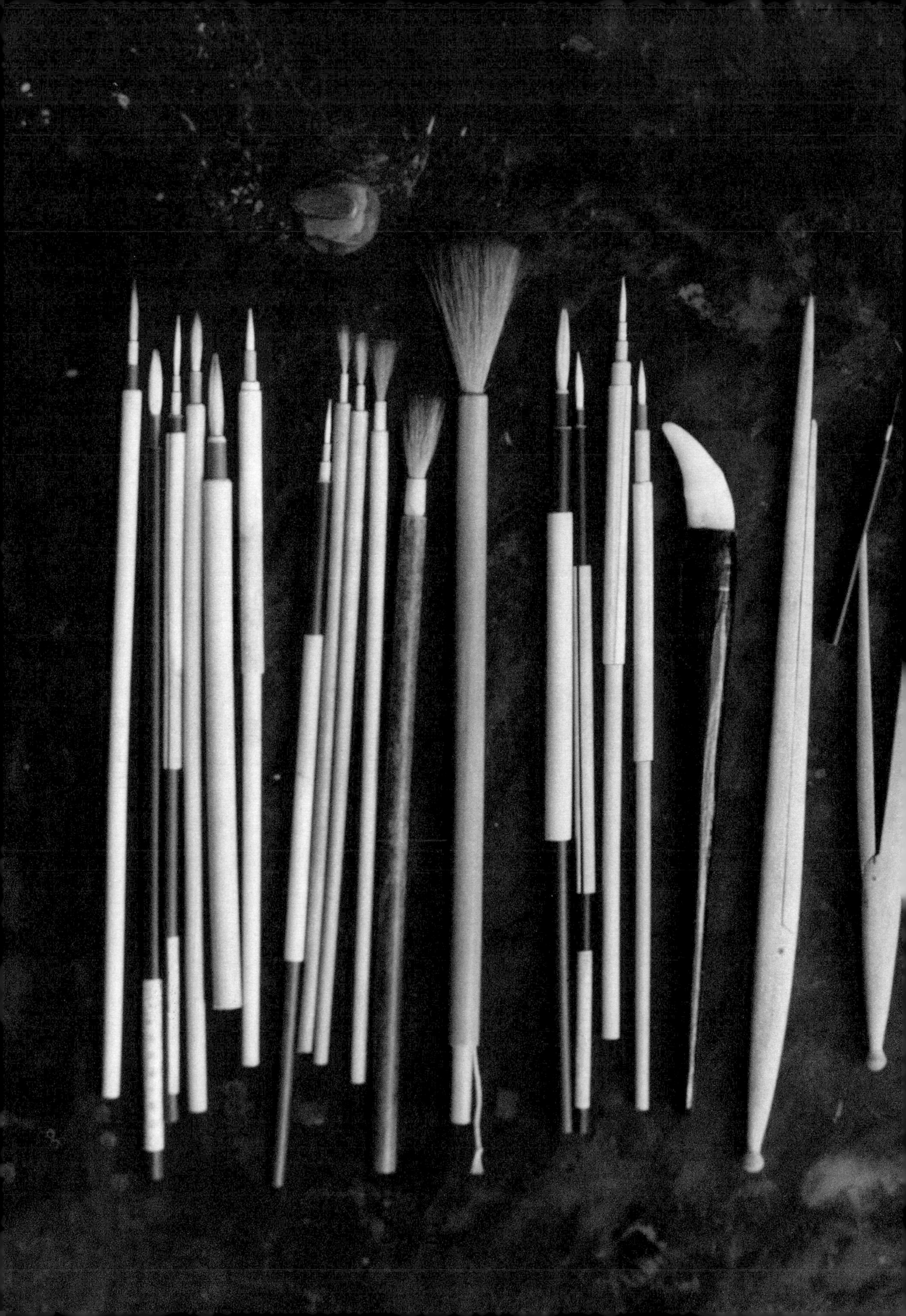

ジョンソン
プリクリー・ヒート
パウダー

高野松山

SHOZAN TAKANO

Modernist in Maki-e

Like Gonroku Matsuda (pages 126–31), Shozan Takano is a master of the *maki-e* technique. Again like Matsuda, he began the study of lacquer while he was still a boy, but he came to his real career as a lacquer artist only after a series of Bohemian escapades that included a sojourn in Manchuria, where, he says, "I became a bandit," and a period (back home in Japan) posing as a mendicant priest during which, he says again, "I nearly landed in jail in Kyoto." Hardship was a commonplace of his existence, but it taught him the patience and self-confidence that were to make him a master of his craft.

His devotion to the art of *maki-e* is complete. Through diligent study he has learned, for example, that more than four hundred different *maki-e* techniques can be distinguished in the decorations of sword sheaths from the Momoyama period. He has been no less diligent in improving the tools of his craft, and he uses a fantastic number of them—more than a thousand in all.

In evolving his own intricate style of *maki-e,* Takano has undeniably been guided by tradition, but he has never allowed its shadow to obscure his individuality. Nor have his highly developed methods led him to a display of mere virtuosity in his work. A lively imagination and a modern sense of design have enabled him to create an unmistakable Takano style.

Although his work has long since been granted the recognition it deserves (he was named a living national treasure in 1955), Takano is by no means satisfied. Looking back over his seventy-eight years of life, he says: "I could have done much more if I had had the means to do it. It takes more than an award and a token allowance to preserve cultural properties. There must be more serious planning if traditional crafts are not to be lost forever." He does not say this in bitterness, but one detects a note of deep sadness when he adds: "There is still so much to be done."

✦

The flower vase on which Takano is at work in the facing photograph simulates a section of bamboo. The intricate pattern is typical of his style. On pages 134–35 he is at work on the lid of a tiny lacquer box whose inside decoration employs infinitely small flakes of gold leaf embedded in wet lacquer. These are cut from the piece at left. The incense container in clam-shell shape (page 136) and the ornamental box with a quail in low relief (page 137) are two of Takano's *maki-e* masterpieces. Page 138 shows a section of his work table with a small receptacle for wet lacquer which he slips over his thumb when he is doing extremely fine work. On page 139 he is again at work on the flower vase of simulated bamboo.

音丸耕堂

KODO OTOMARU

Artist in Choshitsu

The lacquer technique called *choshitsu* requires no less skill than that of *maki-e,* but in this case designs are produced either by carving through layers of lacquer in different colors or by inlaying various colors in an engraved lacquer surface. Originally introduced from China, it was brought to a peak of excellence in the Edo period by Tamakaji Zokoku, whose name has been given to both the special methods that he developed and the lacquer ware he created—that is, Zokoku lacquer. Kodo Otomaru is the finest modern exponent of the *choshitsu* technique.

Otomaru was born in Takamatsu, on the island of Shikoku, where Zokoku himself had lived and worked. Although Zokoku had been dead for three decades when Otomaru was born in 1898, the renown of his work had only continued to grow, and it was almost inevitable that Otomaru should begin his career in lacquer by copying Zokoku's style. It was not long, however, before his individuality asserted itself, and his mastery of the *choshitsu* technique, though firmly grounded in a century-old tradition, is now recognized as a creative achievement of his own. He was named a living national treasure in 1955.

Otomaru makes no bones about the exigencies of his work. "I cannot leave things to chance," he says. "Even when I am applying the layers of lacquer in different colors, I must think about the final design. I must remember the colors and the order in which they are applied, and when I carve, there are all sorts of problems. It is very difficult to do a perfect job, for the lacquer itself is hard and resistant, and carving too deeply or shallowly will not do. Balance is everything, and one must have complete control of the knife." Speed, of course, is the last thing that Otomaru could possibly imagine as an element of his work. "The best time of all," he says, "is the time when I am planning a new design. It takes patience to make it come out the way I want it to, but I am happiest when I have a clear vision of what I want to create."

✦

Otomaru does his own carving of the wooden bases for his creations (facing page). There is nothing particularly strange about the idea that he should use one of his feet as well as well as his hands, for physical control is the essence of his work. The superb quatrefoil design he is carving on pages 142–43 is representative of his finest pieces. Here the carving is done through several layers of lacquer on a monochrome ground. The *tebako* (odds-and-ends box) on page 144, with its cloverleaf pattern centered by tiny clam shells, is done by the same method. Its pleasing shape, no less than its decoration, reveals the skill with which Otomaru employs a traditional technique to create a modern design. The attractions of the tea caddy on page 145 hardly require comment, but it is rather astonishing to learn that it too is a product of the *choshitsu* carving technique—as enticing to hold in one's hands as it to look at.

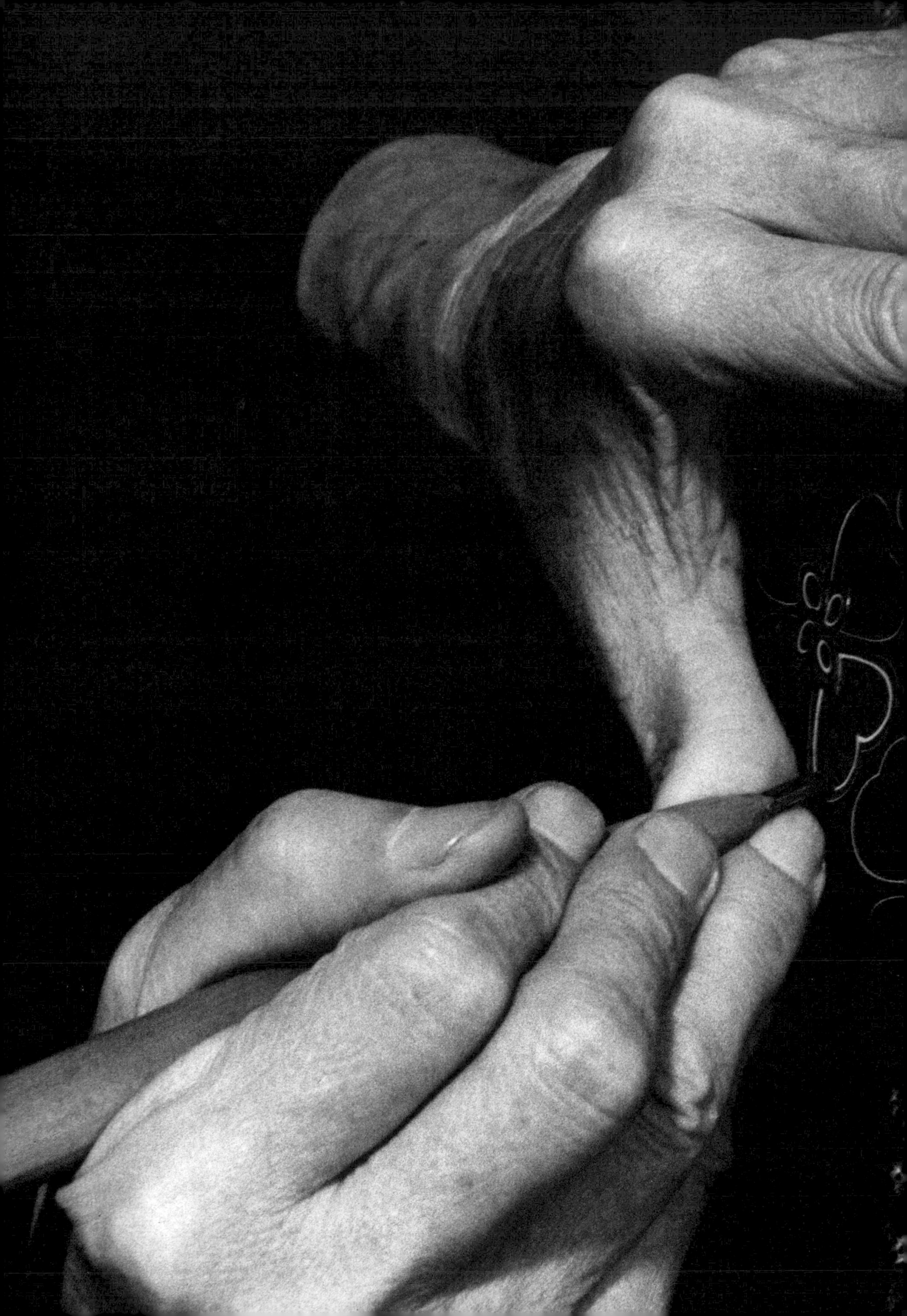

前大峰

TAIHO MAE

Master of the Chinkin Technique

The small city of Wajima, in Ishikawa Prefecture, is a fishing port on the Sea of Japan. This fact alone, of course, gives it no special distinction among the cities of Japan, but Wajima has long been noted for its lacquer ware and particularly for the type of lacquer decoration known as *chinkin* or gold inlay. In this process, imported from China during the Muromachi period, designs carved in the dried lacquer surface are brushed with wet lacquer and filled with gold foil, which is then pressed down by rubbing to make it adhere. The technique has been a tradition of the Wajima lacquerers for several centuries.

Taiho Mae was born to a farm family on the outskirts of Wajima, but he decided quite early that he was not going to be a farmer himself. While he was still in his teens, he left the farm, knocked at the door of the Wajima lacquer artist Sesshu Hashimoto, became his apprentice, and studied with him for five years. He soon discovered that the art of lacquer was not the easy thing he had thought it to be, and he realized that not even two or three decades of work and study would necessarily make him a genuine artist. Mastery of traditional techniques came first, but eventually he was developing new methods of his own. Notable among these was a method of shading that gave a three-dimensional effect instead of the rather flat appearance of the usual *chinkin* decoration.

Taeho Mae is a large man with the stout figure of a *sumo* wrestler, and there is some cause for wonderment when one contrasts the amazing delicacy and complexity of his work with the man himself. He is a familiar figure in Wajima, and even taxi drivers know where he lives. Like the other citizens of the town, they are immensely proud of him, and they have no reservations about letting the visitor know this.

Mae's outstanding achievement is not merely that he has preserved the traditional techniques of Wajima *chinkin* lacquer but also that he has reinvigorated them through the invention of new decorative methods and designs. It was for his attainments in this style of lacquer that he was designated a living national treasure in 1955.

✦

On the opposite page, Taiho Mae (at right) engages in a discussion with one of the men who supply his raw materials. His workshop has a distinctly old-fashioned air, which is accentuated by the antique clock on the wall. The detail of one of his lacquer boxes shown on page 148 epitomizes the delicacy of his work and at the same time displays the three-dimensional effect achieved by his unique method of shading. The box is owned by the National Commission for the Protection of Cultural Properties. On page 149, Mae demonstrates the carving of a design in a dried lacquer surface. His carving tools (page 150) include a wide variety of chisels as well as a modern-style auger.

金工

THE ART OF THE METAL CRAFTSMAN

The long history of metalcraft in Japan appears to have begun before the end of the Stone Age, and a mixed stone-and-metal culture is thought to have preceded the true Metal Age. Among the earliest examples of Japanese metal art that survive today are bronze swords and halberds and the curious bronze objects called *dotaku,* which are assumed to have been bells for ceremonial use and are notable for their lively and sophisticated decoration. Objects like these reveal that the techniques of casting and engraving were well advanced even in such early times, and there is evidence that the more complicated technique of damascene had also been acquired.

With the introduction of Buddhism in the sixth century and the greater importation of techniques from the Asian continent, metalcraft made remarkable strides, particularly in the production of Buddhist ornaments and utensils. During the Nara period (eighth century) casting methods became highly developed, and carving and engraving techniques advanced to the point where they were capable of elaborate and often extremely delicate effects. The bronze Yakushi triad (the Buddha of Healing and two Bodhisattvas) in the Yakushi-ji, one of the oldest temples of Nara, is representative of the high level attained by the metal art of the period.

The Yakushi triad, of course, comes under the heading of sculpture rather than that of metalcraft as we are considering it here, but it expresses the essence of the metal art of the times. Although most Japanese sculpture of the ancient and medieval periods was done in wood or lacquer, since these materials were far more readily available than bronze, it is noteworthy that bronze sculpture on a heroic scale was produced even as early as the Nara period. In addition to the Yakushi triad, we may mention the Great Buddha of the Todai-ji, cast in bronze and dedicated at Nara in 752. Fires and natural calamities, followed by rather uninspired repairs, have left it far less a work of art than it must originally have been, but even today one can gain an idea of the stupendous undertaking that was required to produce it.

At the same we should note that the casting of massive bronze temple bells was already well advanced in the Nara period. Small-scale works in metal were also produced in considerable numbers, largely for purposes of Buddhist ritual. In fact, it would be difficult to overestimate the influence of Buddhism on the metal arts of the Nara and Heian periods.

The rapid refinement of metalcraft techniques continued throughout the Heian period (ninth to late twelfth century), still centering on the production of Buddhist images and ritual objects but also expanding in the manufacture of metal mirrors, swords, and other more profane items. A reliquary for the mythical ashes of the Buddha, preserved in the Saidai-ji at Nara, illustrates the superb skill of the Heian metal artists.

The succeeding Kamakura period (late twelfth to mid-fourteenth century) might well be called the golden age of the Japanese sword. With the collapse of the Heian aristocracy and the rise of the warrior class, the manufacture of armor and weapons took precedence over all other forms of metalcraft, and many of the techniques evolved during this period remain unsurpassed today. It was not only the age of celebrated swordsmiths but also the age of master craftsmen in sword decoration, and it saw the establishment of such renowned metalworking families as those of Goto and Kinya. The Goto craftsmen became particularly famous for their *menuki,* finely wrought plaques that adorned hilts and scabbards; the Kinya artists, for their *tsuba,* the sword guards placed between hilt and blade.

Although fine swords and sword ornaments continued to be made in the following Muromachi period (which saw even more warfare than the days of Kamakura), it is not swords but teakettles that come to mind when we think of Muromachi metalcraft. The reason, of course, is that this period saw the refinement of the tea ceremony into a ritual of art and that the iron teakettle was thereby elevated to a position of importance. Techniques of metalcasting had reached a high level of development, and the Muromachi teakettles were made by pouring liquid pig iron or iron sand (magnetite) into the opening between two earthen molds, the outer one carved on its inner side with superb decorative designs. Most famous among the kettles of this period were those of Ashiya, in Kyushu, and the *temmyo* kettles made in Shimotsuke Province (now Tochigi Prefecture). The Ashiya kettles were distinguished by their smooth texture and delicate decorations in the style of Chinese ink painting, while the works of the *temmyo* craftsmen displayed a rough and masculine quality. The patronage of the Ashikaga shoguns and their popularization of the tea ceremony were outstanding factors in the development of this phase of Muromachi metal art.

In metalcraft, as well as in the other handicraft arts, the Momoyama period (late sixteenth century) tended to stress sheer gorgeousness at the expense of almost everything else. The military dictators Nobunaga and Hideyoshi created conditions that favored the rise of an affluent merchant class, not only through the development of commercial towns but also through the expansion of foreign trade. The merchant class had little use for the purely traditional in the arts and crafts. Their taste was for the new, the lively, and the gorgeous, and in this they were encouraged by the examples of Nobunaga and Hideyoshi themselves, who built magnificent castles and decorated them in magnificent style. Not only the metal accessories of interior decoration but also weapons and armor reflected the trend, and even the lowly teakettle began to put on airs.

The two and a half centuries of the Edo period, which began around 1600, brought further elaborations in metalcraft techniques and design, often stressing ornamentation, especially in armor and swords, to the exclusion of usefulness. Nevertheless, a few metal craftsmen practiced restraint and were able to create works of refinement and artistic style. The Goto craftsmen adhered to the excellent traditions established by their ancestors in the Kamakura period, and such genuine artists as Yokoya Somin, Nara Toshihisa, Tsuchiya Yasuchika, and Sugimura Joi brought distinction to the craft.

From its beginnings in the late Stone Age down to the advent of Japan's modern period in the second half of the nineteenth century, the art of the metal craftsman produced an infinite variety of objects both for decoration and for daily use. To name only a few, besides those already noted, we may mention such tea-ceremony utensils as the charcoal brazier and the water bowl, such art objects as incense burners and sculptures for the tokonoma, such religious accessories as temple bells and gongs, and such personal articles as jewelry and seals. In a word, the handmade products of Japan's metal artists once played an intimate role in the everyday life of the people.

Today, however, all this has changed. Swords and sword furnishings have long since gone the way of metal mirrors and helmets, even though the craft of swordmaking, as we shall presently see, has not vanished completely. Many of the metal articles formerly made by hand are now produced by machine, and many have been replaced by products made of other materials. This is not to say that there is no longer a demand for the hand-crafted products of Japan's metal artists, but the demand is small, and the cost of such products is necessarily high. It is heartening, in any case, to know that the traditions of Japanese metalcraft have not been entirely discarded.

The traditional tea-ceremony kettle, for example, has by no means succumbed to the dominance of the machine. It is still made by hand in a surprising variety of textures and shapes, and it manages very well to preserve its antique charm. Many of the shapes are new, but they nevertheless reflect a respect for traditional values. Among such teakettles we may mention those in the shape of bottle gourds, melons, and Mount Fuji and even some which are square. The designs with which they are ornamented are no less elegant than those of the Muromachi kettles, even when they are most conspicuously modern.

The swords of Japan deserve a paragraph or two to themselves, not only because of their fame as weapons but also because of the superlative artistry that went into their making. Although their age of glory is long since past, a few of them are still made today as art objects, and it is fortunate indeed that the craft and its techniques have not been lost.

The forging of the blade was of course the most important step in the process, since a sword must be hard and razor sharp but not brittle enough to break, and complicated welding and tempering techniques had to be evolved. The natural designs produced during these processes are of remarkable beauty in themselves, and control of the processes could be used to achieve varying effects in the finished blades—patterns, for example, that resembled waves, flames, trees, and the like. Sometimes the blades were decorated with engraving or gold inlay. At the same time great care was given to the decoration of the hilt and the scabbard and to the design of the sword guard placed between the hilt and the blade. Thus other metal craftsmen besides the swordsmith himself were involved in creating the total effect. Today only a few of these craftsmen are at work, but they are as fully dedicated to their craft as the swordsmiths are to theirs, and one can only be grateful that the art of the Japanese sword survives, even though it is a precarious survival at best.

The five men who make up the roster of living treasures among Japan's metal craftsmen are the swordsmiths Sadatsugu Takahashi and Akihira Miyairi, the maker of sword guards Tahei Yonemitsu, the teakettle maker Tetsushi Nagano, and the metalcaster Toyochika Takamura. Death has removed three other artists from the roster. They were Kiyoshi Unno, honored for his exquisite techniques of casting; Shodo Sasaki, who was a master of lost-wax casting; and Iraku Uozumi, maker of temple gongs.

高橋貞次

SADATSUGU TAKAHASHI

Swordmaker of Matsuyama

Swordmaking has long been regarded as the most important of all the Japanese metalworking arts. In fact, it is commonly placed in a category by itself, and traditionally it was treated more as a ritual than as a craft. With the rise of the warrior class in the twelfth century, there developed a cult of the sword that survived well into Japan's modern period, and the sword indeed became the soul of the samurai, as the Japanese saying has it, for it served as an emblem of the valor and honor of the warrior. Great swords of the past, particularly from the Kamakura period, are revered as works of art, and some one hundred of them are registered as national art treasures.

It is important to know all this when one comes to consider the work of Sadatsugu Takahashi, swordmaker of Matsuyama, in Shikoku, for he is one of the very few followers of the craft today. He came to it while the sword was still an accessory of the Japanese military man, though somewhat more ornamental than utilitarian in a day of guns and bombs. That day is now more than a quarter of a century past, but Takahashi remains loyal to his art. His training began under the famous swordsmith Sadakatsu Gassan some fifty years ago. Since 1923, when he established his own workshop in Matsuyama, he has risen to the top position among Japan's remaining swordmakers, and in 1955 he was honored by being named a living national treasure.

Takahashi is a man of great reserve and dignity, and one immediately senses in him a consuming dedication to the art of the sword. He is also a strict traditionalist, adhering even to the ceremonial aspect of his craft, which regards the swordsmith as a priest, his workshop as a shrine, and the forging of a sword as a religious rite. His blades take their inspiration from famous swords of the past, but his style is indisputably his own. He is as well known for his decorative designs as for the excellence of the blades on which he engraves them, and his interpretations of such traditional sword symbols as the dragon and the god Fudo are noted for their elegance and grace.

✦

The sign at the gate of Takahashi's house (page 157) announces his name, his title of living national treasure, and his honorary title of Ryusen, swordmaker. On pages 158–59 he sits before his forge in the ritual costume of the old-time swordsmith, an anvil in front of him, a hammer in his right hand, and a newly forged blade in his left. The sledgehammers at right are used in early stages of the forging. Page 160 shows Takahashi engraving a blade with a symbolic dragon design. The finished blade on page 161 is engraved with a typical Takahashi dragon and inscribed with his professional name Ryusen Sadatsugu and the date on which the work was completed.

高橋貞次
龍王子・龍泉

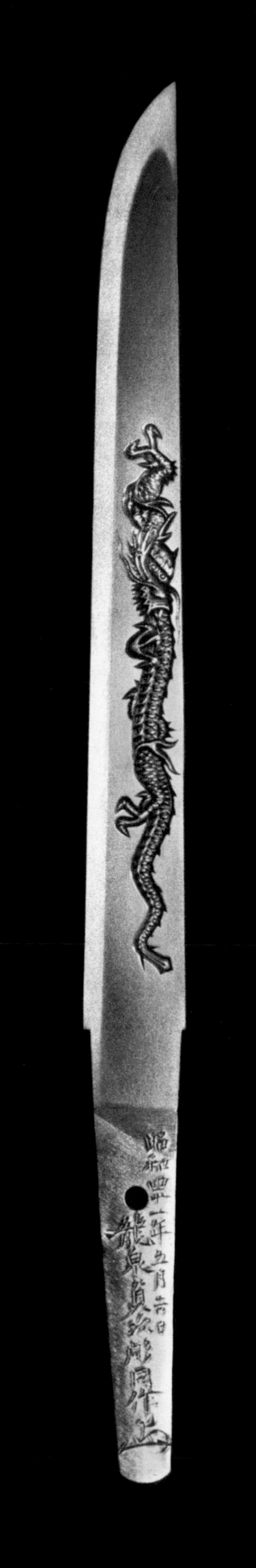

米光太平

TAHEI YONEMITSU

Maker of Sword Guards

An important part of a Japanese sword is the *tsuba:* the metal plate or guard placed at the point where the tang of the blade enters the hilt. Sword guards have traditionally been regarded as objects of art in themselves, and today they are treasured by collectors as examples of Japanese metalcraft in one of its most attractive forms. Since fine swords are still made, fine sword guards are also produced today, but the craft, like that of the swordsmith, has barely managed to survive.

Tahei Yonemitsu is one of the few remaining makers of sword guards. He was born in Kumamoto Prefecture, in Kyushu, where the metalcraft techniques of damascene and openwork had been practiced for centuries. The old name of this region was Higo, and its metal artists attained such renown that their work went by such names as Higo damascene and Higo openwork. Their iron sword guards, carved into unique designs and tastefully inlaid with gold, were the most famous products of their craft, and it was this craft that Yonemitsu learned from his grandfather in the early years of the present century. He is thus the successor to traditional Higo techniques that found their most fluent expression in feudal days. To bring these techniques to life again in modern times was a distinguished achievement in itself, but to use them in the creation of a new and individual style was no less significant. For both of these accomplishments Yonemitsu was designated a living national treasure in 1965.

The visitor to his workshop in Kumamoto City may be somewhat startled to see a group of young apprentices at work not on sword guards but on tie clips, cuff links, and belt buckles—all of them employing traditional Higo techniques to create modern designs. "I never teach these young men to make sword guards until they have spent ten years on these other things," says Yonemitsu. "I know they want to create something outstanding in a hurry, but they must learn patience and obedience first." The young apprentices, it seems, are not unhappy about this arrangement. Perhaps among them there will be a worthy successor to the master, but one wonders whether he will be making sword guards or costume jewelry.

✦

Yonemitsu's workshop (facing page) is part of his house, and this is no doubt why it has a rather warm and domestic air. Here he is seen applying damascene inlay to one of his sword guards. The newly cut guard and the assortment of his tools on pages 164–65 express the spirit of his craftsmanship: nothing mechanical, everything by hand, and a deep concern with basic design. Page 166 shows six steps in the creation of a Yonemitsu sword guard, from raw metal through cutting and polishing to application of the inlay. The central opening, of course, fits the blade of the sword. The graceful masterpiece on page 167 (owned by the National Commission for the Protection of Cultural Properties) is decorated with peony arabesques in gold damascene and bears the artist's signature.

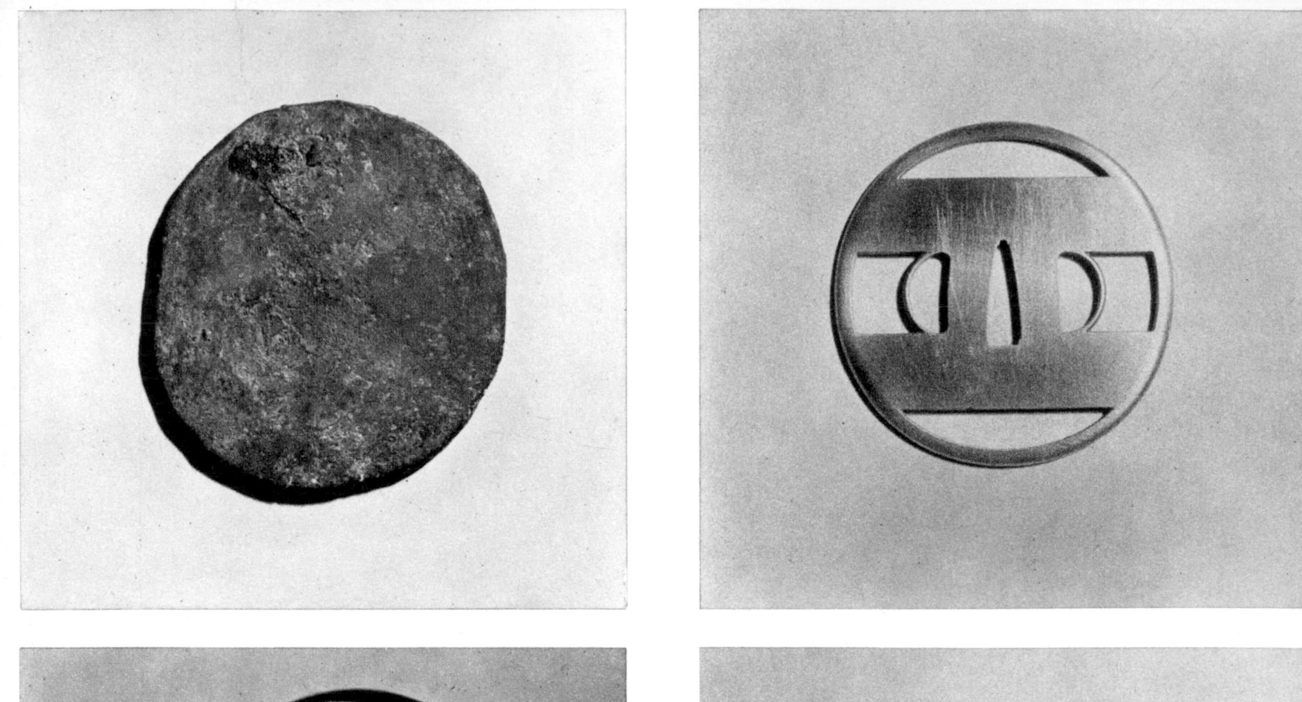
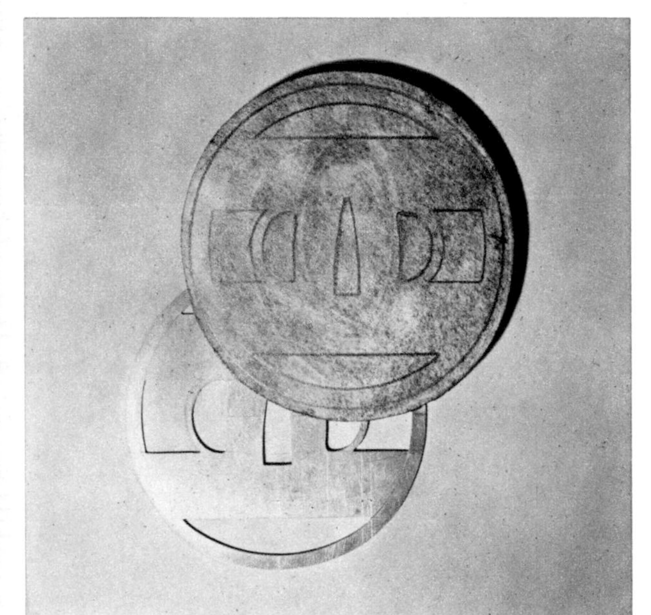

肥後
米光太平安之

宮入昭平

AKIHIRA MIYAIRI

Swordmaker of Nagano

Akihira Miyairi comes from a long line of swordsmiths. He was born in Nagano Prefecture, and it is there that he follows his craft today. With his father as teacher, he began his apprenticeship after finishing elementary school. The skill he displayed was phenomenal, and even as a young man he was listed among expert swordmakers. His swords won prize after prize in national competitions, and in 1963, at the age of fifty, he was named a living national treasure. When one considers the great length of time required to forge a fine blade, it seems remarkable that Miyairi has some three hundred swords to his credit.

His style derives mainly from two great traditions laid down in the Kamakura period, when swordmaking reached its zenith in Japan: the traditions established by Masamune, perhaps the most revered of all Japanese swordmakers, and by Masamune's disciple Kaneuji. Combining the best elements in the work of these two masters, Miyairi has evolved an artistry peculiarly his own. It is difficult to describe the essence of his work, but elegance and a certain serene beauty are decidedly part of it.

Miyairi works with a partner and four young apprentices, one of whom is an American who came to Japan to learn the craft. Life is rigorous for the apprentices, for they work from dawn until long past dusk, not only assisting in the swordmaking process itself but also cutting charcoal for the forge, cleaning the workshop, and performing other chores. Since Miyairi insists that the secrets of swordmaking can be learned only by "mind"—that is, intense concentration—the forging of a blade is carried on in silence but with the complete harmony of all the participants. The apprentices, in a word, understand and anticipate every movement of the master during the forging process.

✦

The Miyairi house (facing page) is typical of rural houses in traditional style. At left is the workshop; in the foreground, a dugout for storing charcoal. Since the forging process is considered a ritual, the entrance to the workshop (page 170) is decorated with a sacred straw rope of the type hung at the entrance to a Shinto shrine. The hammering out of a white-hot blade (page 171) requires completely coordinated movement by the three assistants while the master adjusts its position on the anvil. All are appropriately costumed for the ritual. Tempering (pages 172–73) requires repeated heating and cooling of the blade and applications of wet clay to produce a hard-tempered cutting edge and a soft-tempered back. Pages 174–75 picture the dramatic moment when the repeatedly heated and beaten metal of the clay-covered blade finally resolves into clean, hard steel. The patterned arrangement of the clay is designed to produce a pattern in the blade. On page 176, Miyairi engraves his signature on the tang of a finished blade.

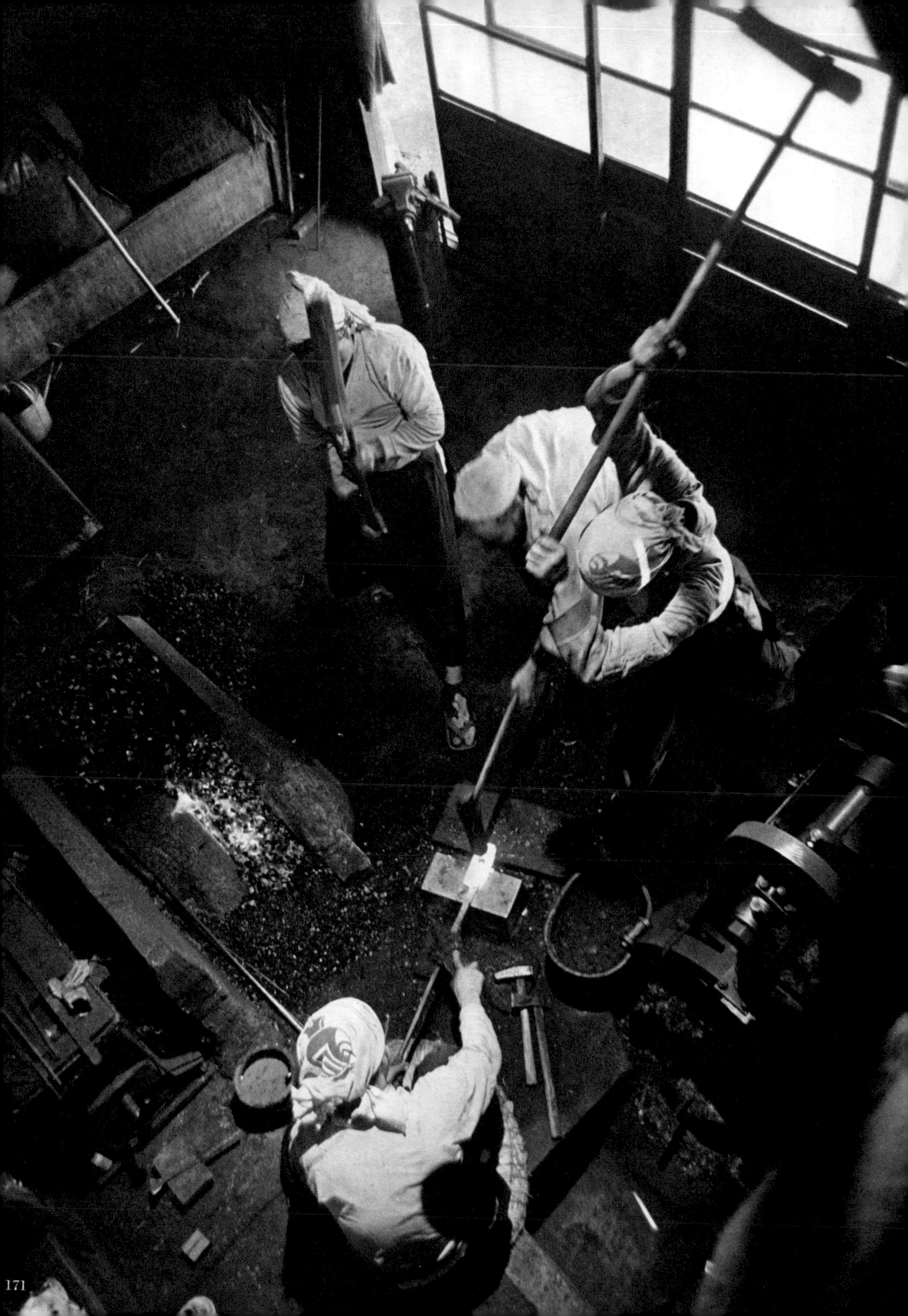

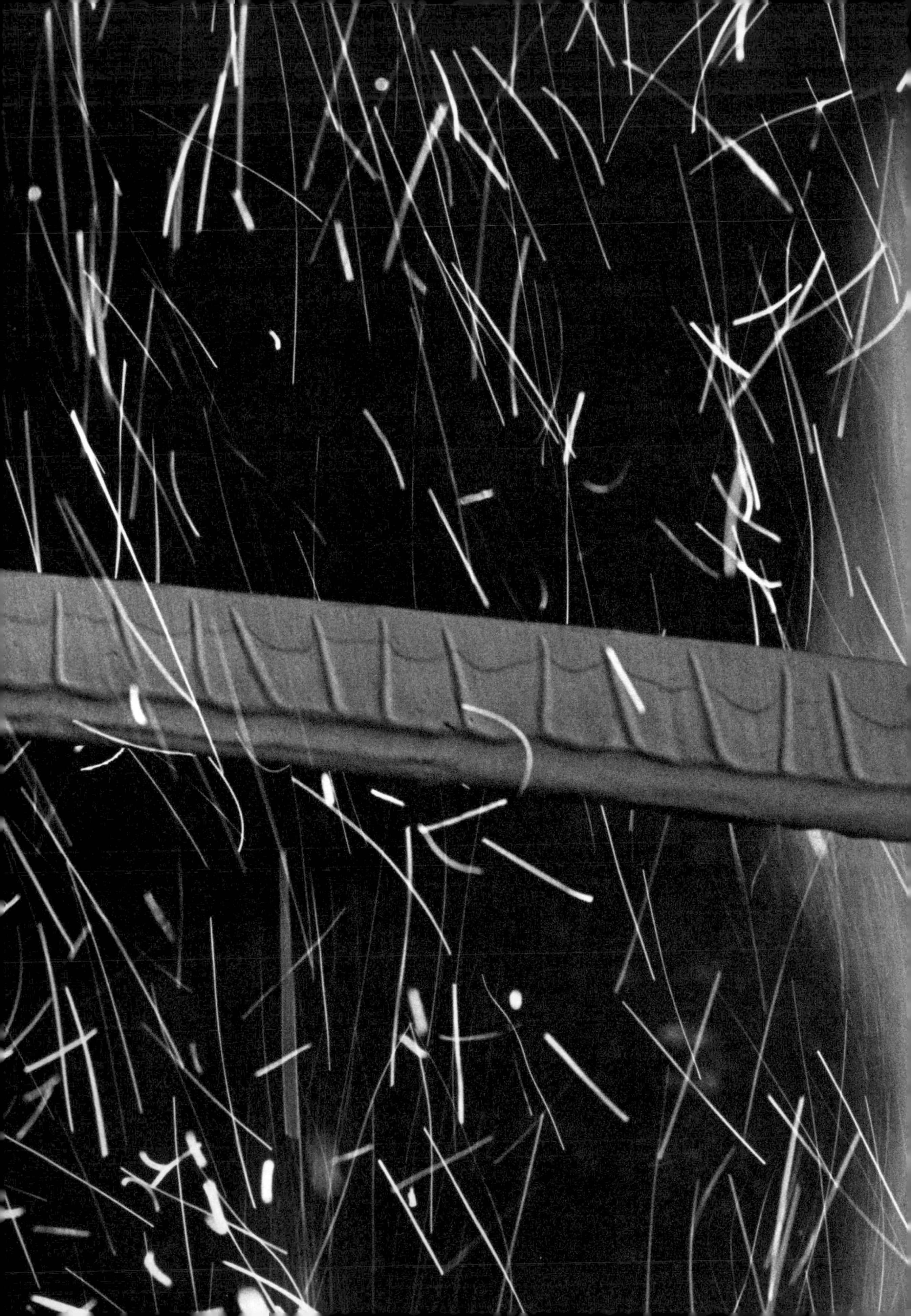

長野垤志

TETSUSHI NAGANO

Maker of Ceremonial Teakettles

No less important to the tea ceremony than pottery tea bowls is the kettle in which water is boiled to make the tea. Traditionally such kettles have always been made of iron, a sober and unpretentious metal whose color and texture meet very well the canon of rustic simplicity laid down for the tearoom and its furnishings. Since the tea ceremony survives today in traditional form, the iron teakettle has survived along with it, and the kettles of master craftsmen are still highly prized.

One of these master craftsmen is Tetsushi Nagano, who lives in Tokyo but makes his teakettles in the northern city of Yamagata, where metalcasting has a long tradition. Nagano is not satisfied with easy methods and materials. While most of today's craftsmen use pig iron for their kettles because it is easier to work with, he insists on using iron sand (magnetite), which is difficult to handle because it solidifies quickly during casting. But he has good reasons for his choice. Iron sand gives a superb texture and color and enables the metalcaster to produce kettles with thinner walls and therefore more lightness and grace. At the same time, such kettles are far more durable than those made with pig iron. Nevertheless, about one out of three iron-sand kettles is likely to crack in cooling, regardless of Nagano's skill in casting.

Nagano's techniques are traditional, but his sense of design is modern. Even so, his teakettles convey the same impression of quiet elegance and rustic sturdiness that one finds in those of earlier days. He has long been recognized as a master of his craft, and in 1963 he was honored for this mastery by being designated a living national treasure.

✦

On the facing page Nagano works on one of his earthen molds with the same intense concentration that he gives to every other aspect of his craft. The mold on page 180 is for a teakettle of the same type as that shown on page 184. The only decorations are the stylized bouquets at the points where the handle will be inserted. During casting, the mold is held firm by the use of the old-style *makka* supports seen on page 181. Nagano (at right) is an expert judge of exactly the right amount of molten iron to be poured into the mold and exactly the right moment to pour it. On pages 182–83, Nagano (foreground) and an assistant put the finishing touches to newly cast kettles by adding handles and lids. The two spoutless kettles on the following pages are examples of Nagano's tea-ceremony kettles at their most elegant, the one (page 184) in classical style with decorations of stylized bouquets and a flower motif on its lid, the other (page 185) distinctly modern, with stylized woodpeckers as handle supports and a pleasingly shaped knob on the lid.

高村豊周

TOYOCHIKA TAKAMURA

Artist in Metalcasting

While Tetsushi Nagano (pages 178–85) casts his ceremonial teakettles in iron sand, Toyochika Takamura uses the more sophisticated materials of copper and copper-silver alloy to create flower vases and various other pieces of ornamental metalware. There is no essential difference in their motives, however, for each is intent upon preserving a traditional craft by enlivening it with a modern sense of design.

Takamura comes from a distinguished artistic background. His father was the famous sculptor Koun Takamura, and his elder brother, Kotaro, is noted both as a sculptor and as a poet. It is hardly surprising to note that Takamura, in addition to having achieved renown in metalcasting, is a well-known poet himself. In fact, his literary talent seems to be reflected in the grace and elegance of his metal creations, which decidedly have a poetry of their own.

In his casting, Takamura uses the *cire-perdue* or lost-wax method. In this process an inner mold of clay is covered with a layer of wax, then with another layer of clay to form the outer mold, and finally with still another layer of clay into which fragments of unglazed pottery are pressed to produce special effects in the surface of the cast object. Metal pins running from the inner mold through the wax and the outer mold serve to hold the two molds in place during casting. The whole construction is then heated, so that the wax runs out and leaves an empty space into which molten metal is poured. The outer and inner molds are then shattered to free the cast object.

Finishing a cast object takes much longer than the casting itself. First, the holes left by the pins are filled with metal. The surface is then polished, and the cast object is reheated to produce a pleasing texture. Another polishing follows, and repeated applications of special dyes are used to produce various colors.

It goes without saying that Takamura is a master of this technique. He has used it to create forms which not only emphasize the characteristics of his material but also display an interesting harmony between traditional inspiration and modern creative design. For these achievements he was named a living national treasure in 1964.

✦

On the facing page, Takamura works on one of his molds at his Tokyo workshop. He insists on a clean separation between conception of a design and actual production, and he never begins a new piece until he knows exactly what he wants it to be. Pages 188–89 show four of the molds described above: three outer molds and another with its coating of clay and fragments of pottery. The molten metal is poured in through the tubes. The flower container of copper-silver alloy on page 190 typifies Takamura's superb sense of design. It is owned by the National Commission for the Protection of Cultural Properties.

竹芸

THE ART OF THE BAMBOO CRAFTSMAN

It is perhaps not strange that there should be only one bamboo craftsman among Japan's living national treasures. Bamboo, like wood, has been used for so many commonplace articles of everyday life that the bamboo craftsman has rarely been considered the equal of the potter, the lacquerer, or the metal craftsman. Again, articles made of bamboo (or of wood) are generally far less durable than those made of "hard" materials, and it is rather difficult to consider them as works of art. Nevertheless, there is an art of bamboo in Japan, and it has existed since ancient times.

It is not until the eighth century, however, that we have clear evidence of what early Japanese bamboo work was like. Among the treasures of the Shoso-in, at Nara, there are bamboo swords, bamboo musical instruments, and bamboo writing brushes. There are also baskets of split bamboo and boxes inlaid with mosaics of thinly cut bamboo stained in different colors. All of these show their great age and have suffered from natural deterioration, but they reveal quite clearly that the bamboo craftsmen of the time were already using quite sophisticated techniques.

The Nara-period treasures of the Shoso-in were preserved by marvelous good fortune, escaping the fires and natural calamities that destroyed all other examples of bamboo work from that distant age. From succeeding ages, at least down to comparatively modern times, hardly any examples of such work exist. We know, of course, that bamboo continued to be a favorite material for articles of everyday use, but for the most part these articles were considered disposable and of no real artistic value.

In the sixteenth century, when the tea ceremony reached a climax of refinement under the inspiration of the master Sen no Rikyu, bamboo acquired a new aesthetic significance. Sen, in an effort to do away with ostentation in the tearoom, dictated the canon of elegant plainness and, in addition to choosing tea bowls of rustic cast, used a section of bamboo as a container for the simple flower arrangement that decorated the tokonoma. The ivory spoons introduced from China in the early days of the tea cult were replaced with spoons of bamboo, and tea-ceremony masters found new beauty in the unpretentious works of anonymous bamboo craftsmen.

In time, a number of bamboo artists emerged into prominence as producers of tea-ceremony accessories. Among them were Kuroda Shogen, who studied the tea ceremony under the master Kobori Enshu and acquired the technique of making bamboo spoons that seemed to express the essence of what tea masters were seeking. Other craftsmen became famous for their bamboo tea whisks (for whipping the powdered green tea to a froth when boiling water was added) and their bamboo flower vases. In fact, it was largely the tea ceremony that raised the work of bamboo craftsmen to the level of an art in modern times.

The bamboo craftsman uses his material in two basic ways: either as whole sections cut from the long stems of the plant (for flower vases and the like) or as thin strips of the outer skin (for baskets and other woven forms). No bamboo technique is as simple as it looks, since, first of all, the material must be carefully selected according to such qualities as age, soundness, and color. Again, when sections of bamboo are used for vases and similar articles, shape is an important consideration. Sometimes green bamboo is used, chiefly for disposable baskets and other containers, but more frequently the bamboo is aged, especially for the making of decorative objects. Sometimes it is smoked or stained to change its color. Articles of woven bamboo appear in a multiplicity of shapes and patterns, and these vary from district to district throughout the country.

The number of bamboo craftsmen in Japan is beyond counting, for their products are still in wide and constant use. But, as we have already noted, it is hardly strange that only one of these craftsmen should be listed among the living national treasures, for very few of them are truly artists in bamboo.

生野祥雲斎

SHOUNSAI SHONO

Artist in Bamboo

The prefecture of Oita, in Kyushu, is noted not only for the quality of its bamboo but also for its long tradition in bamboo handicrafts. Shounsai Shono was born in this region and continues to work there today as the foremost of Japan's bamboo craftsmen. It must be emphasized, however, that he is far more than an artisan carrying on a traditional craft, for he has raised the craft to the level of an art. This was his ambition when he finished his apprenticeship, and he has fulfilled it to perfection.

Although Shono at first intended to be either a painter or a sculptor, ill health forced him into a different vocation. From early childhood he had been fascinated by the beauty of bamboo, and when he realized that he must earn his living by a relatively placid occupation, it seemed natural to turn to bamboo as a craft. He once wrote: "We must never forget to show our sincere admiration and our appreciation of the beauty of bamboo. Only those who can retain the fresh spirit of the living bamboo in their work are worthy to be called true craftsmen."

Shono insists on going to the bamboo grove to select his own material and on supervising every step of its preparation for use, for he feels that the relationship between himself and the material should be an intimate one from start to finish. Through his admirable inventiveness he has freed bamboo from its slavery to the tea ceremony and given it a more important role in decoration and utility in the form of graceful baskets and other types of containers. It is his special aim in all his creations to reflect the grace of the living bamboo plant: the elegant curves and the pliability that have made it a favorite theme of Japanese painting. He often gives his works titles that include the word "waves," since this suggests the curves and movement of a windswept bamboo grove. Shono became a living national treasure in 1967, but the attainment of this honor has not changed his way of life. He still occupies the old studio that he established in Oita City years ago, and in this quiet setting, from which he can look out over the Bay of Beppu, he goes on with the work that he has now been doing for almost half a century.

✦

Shounsai Shono (facing page) prefers to sit in traditional style to weave his bamboo baskets. The work requires an assortment of shears and knives as well as a large dish of water to moisten the strips of bamboo from time to time. On page 196 we see the beginning of a favorite Japanese pattern in bamboo weaving: the *ajiro* pattern used for screens, fences, sliding doors, and, of course, baskets. The basket on page 197 gives full expression to Shono's ideals of craftsmanship: grace of design and emphasis on the natural character of the material. On page 198, Shono is seen at the door of his bamboo storehouse. The bamboo, of the species called *madake,* has already been aged and dried and is ready for use.

THE ART OF THE JAPANESE DOLL

It is impossible to say with any certainty just when dolls were first made in Japan. Undoubtedly there were dollmakers in prehistoric times, for we have the evidence of the strange ceramic figurines called *dogu,* which seem to have served as fetishes or fertility symbols. These grotesque images from the Jomon period (around 4000 to around 200 B.C.) were clearly not intended as playthings, but their existence suggests that dolls were also made in the same period.

We are not really on firm ground, however, until we come to the early years of the Heian period (ninth to late twelfth century), and it is safer to trace the history of dollmaking from that time. We know, for example, that dolls served as playthings for both girls and boys during Heian times. In Lady Murasaki's celebrated novel of the eleventh century, *The Tale of Genji,* we find children making and playing with dolls of paper, and in the almost contemporary collection of tales known as the *Konjaku Monogatari* we learn about a "clockwork" doll that could be made to move its head when water was poured into it. We also know that sets of dolls were made for children of the Heian nobility and that this custom evolved into the Doll Festival, which is now celebrated on March 3. It is interesting to note in addition that large doll-like figures of straw were placed at roadsides to ward off epidemics and natural calamities by serving as substitutes for possible human victims. Again, we may note that puppet shows were among the entertainments of Heian society.

Subsequent periods brought the rather naïve dolls of early times to higher and higher levels of sophistication until, in the Edo period (seventeenth to mid-nineteenth century), the craft of the dollmaker reached a climax of achievement. Now the newly risen merchant class established a culture of its own—a culture that produced the *ukiyo-e* woodblock print, the Bunraku theater, and the Kabuki drama—and it was inevitable that these should provide themes for contemporary dollmakers.

Costume dolls had already appeared long before Edo times, but they had never before been made in such variety and profusion. Nor had the materials of dollmaking ever been so numerous or elaborate. Now the dollmakers began to copy characters from the drama—Kabuki, Bunraku, and Noh—and figures from the "floating world" like those which appear in the *ukiyo-e* prints. Dolls of this last type came to be known as *isho ningyo* (costume dolls) and were often called *ukiyo ningyo*—that is, dolls of the floating world. They are still tremendously popular today.

Puppets, we should note, were by no means an invention of the Edo period, nor was the Bunraku theater the only place where they were employed. Many regions had their own versions of the puppet theater, and traveling puppet shows had been common for at least five centuries. But the puppetmakers of Edo times were far ahead of their predecessors in technique and ingenuity, and their finest creations were not only admired as stars of puppet entertainments but also treasured as works of art in their own right.

It is not possible in this brief account to describe the entire range of the dollmaker's art in Edo days, but it will be of interest to mention a few outstanding types of dolls besides those already noted above. Often these dolls were regional products, and a number of districts became famous for specific types.

The Saga dolls of Kyoto were carved from wood and colored with bright paints, their costumes suggesting the exquisite Saga brocade made in that city. Originally this method of painting on carved wood was used in producing Buddhist sculpture, but the decline of Buddhism during the Edo period, along with the increase in dollmaking, caused a number of Buddhist sculptors to turn to the making of Saga dolls. Interestingly enough, the earliest of these dolls strongly resembled Buddhist images, but in time such new themes as the Seven Gods of Good Fortune, children in Chinese costume, and beautiful women of the demimonde were introduced. Gradually, however, the popularity of the Saga dolls faded, and the craft, despite a rather successful revival in the early years of the present century, is almost a lost art today.

Kyoto was also famous for its elegant Kamo dolls, first made in the early eighteenth century as a pastime of priests at the Kamo Shrine. These were also of wood, but only the faces were painted, the costumes being made of real cloth pasted on the wooden form.

Dolls made expressly for the Edo-period nobility were often true works of art with personalities of their own. The *gosho ningyo* (imperial palace dolls), for example, might portray characters from the Noh drama in full costume or engaging young children almost completely in the nude. These dolls were first made of clay and later of painted wood and were particularly noted for their lifelike expressions.

Sets of dolls for the Doll Festival were often quite elaborate and expensive, as they still are today. They were treated as heirlooms and were stored away except for their brief appearance on the third day of March. Even then, however, they were considered as objects for display rather than as toys, and the young girls who owned them were taught to handle them with care. Similarly, the dolls displayed on Boys' Day (May 5) were regarded with a certain reverence, and their role was to inspire the boys of of the family with ideals of manliness and courage rather than to amuse them as playthings. Festival dolls of this type became widely popular in the Edo period, since the merchant class and even the less affluent levels of society could now afford to own them, and they are no less popular today.

Among the purely folkcraft dolls that survive from earlier days, perhaps the best known are the *kokeshi:* cylindrical figures of lathe-turned wood with prominent round heads. These dolls, sometimes quite large and sometimes with movable heads, are painted or lacquered in various ways, usually to suggest people of olden times. The *kokeshi* might be said to represent the ultimate in stylization of the Japanese doll.

The transition from the Edo period to the modern age brought innovations in dollmaking styles and techniques, but a surprising number of dolls continue to be made in traditional fashion. There is a great difference, of course, between those which are mass-produced for the commercial market and those which are the individual works of devoted artists. As in olden times in Japan, most dolls today are made by anonymous craftsmen who produce them to satisfy the popular taste and not to express creative ideas of their own. These dolls, although they often have considerable charm, are nevertheless stereotypes, and this, no doubt, is as it should be. A doll is not expected to be a work of sculpture, let us say, but at most an object of decorative beauty—a means of giving pleasure without inspiring profound aesthetic reactions. At least we can be grateful to the anonymous dollmakers for adding this much brightness to our lives. And yet, the work of a master dollmaker is clearly something different, and the difference is one that we instantly recognize.

At this point we may well stop for a moment and ask ourselves what a doll is really supposed to be. Our first impulse is to say that it is no more than a plaything, but a moment's thought tells us that this answer will not do. In Japan, quite obviously (and in many other countries as well), a doll is not always a plaything, for many dolls are purely decorative objects, as we have already noted. Of course there are Japanese dolls which are meant purely for use as toys, but these are never given the respect accorded the works of master dollmakers in traditional style. In fact, it is here that traditional dollmaking sometimes appears to cross the borderline into sculpture. Actually, however, there is still a difference between sculpture and dollmaking, for sculpture is creative in a way that dollmaking is not. Sculpture, in a word, gives the impression of serious intent, while dollmaking seems always to have the look of a pastime, and indeed many Japanese take it up for that purpose. In any case, few of us would make extravagant claims of sculptural virtues for Japanese dolls even at their most inspired. And yet, sometimes we are not so sure, particularly when we study dolls like those displayed in the photographs that accompany this section of the book. Let us repeat, then, what we have said above: that a doll is essentially a plaything and at best an object of decorative beauty. But let us also say that the best creations of Japan's traditional dollmakers are unmistakably works of art.

The visitor to the doll section of a Japanese department store will be confronted by an array of traditional dolls in great numbers, but few of them indeed will bear the stamp of individuality that marks them as the work of genuine artists. Costume dolls are there by the hundreds, along with *kokeshi* and the famous plaster dolls of Hakata, which copy figures from history, legend, and everyday life. These are only part of the assortment, and one finds Western-style dolls as well. But if the visitor wants to see the finest in traditional dolls, he must go to the art department of the store, for it is there that the creations of Japan's finest dollmakers are found, and they are there because they are regarded as art objects and not as mere playthings or undistinguished pieces of bric-a-brac.

This in turn suggests why dollmakers are included among the craftsmen who are honored as living national treasures. In a word, the craft of dollmaking, no less than the crafts of pottery and weaving, for example, can be a medium of artistic expression, and those who preserve its finest traditions are just as deserving of honor as those who preserve the traditions of other crafts.

Two men and one woman have been named as living national treasures for their outstanding work in the preservation of traditional dollmaking techniques. They are by no means the only true artists among the dollmakers of Japan, but they may be said to symbolize all the craftsmen who bring distinction to the art of the Japanese doll in the present age. Goyo Hirata and Ryujo Hori have devoted years of effort to the *isho ningyo,* the costume doll of carved wood. Juzo Kagoshima has spent most of his life creating *shiso ningyo* or dolls of molded paper. It is not only the technical mastery of these artists that makes them noteworthy; more impressive even than this is their remarkable gift of producing an illusion of life and personality in the dolls they create.

平田郷陽

GOYO HIRATA

Realist of the Costume Doll

Goyo Hirata once defined his ideal as the creation of dolls with the same elegance of line that characterizes the figures in the best of the *ukiyo-e* woodblock prints. This ideal has long since been realized in his work, and he is known today as the foremost master of the costume doll. Traditionally such dolls are made in realistic style, for they often copy characters from the "floating world" of the woodblock prints—for example, actors and beautiful women of the demimonde. Hirata's dolls are quite lifelike, but there is a curious beauty about them that goes beyond mere realism, and it is this that sets them apart from the run of dolls in traditional style.

Hirata was born to a family of dollmakers in the Tokyo entertainment district of Asakusa. After finishing elementary school, he began his apprenticeship under his father, who had studied the craft with Kamehachi Yasumoto, a nineteenth-century master noted for the amazing realism of his dolls. Undoubtedly something of the Yasumoto style and techniques survives today in Hirata's work, but Hirata, however much he may be a servant of tradition, is by no means its slave. His dolls display not only consummate technical skill but also a creative imagination that is peculiarly his own.

Hirata has gone abroad several times to demonstrate the techniques of Japanese dollmaking—for example, at international expositions in Paris, Brussels, and São Paulo—and has participated in countless exhibitions in Japan. He has also formed about him a group of artists who work to preserve the traditions of the craft. The honor of being named a living national treasure came to him in 1955.

✦

The doll on the facing page (owned by the National Commission for the Protection of Cultural Properties) is typical of Hirata's finest work. Here a paint called *gofun* (made of powdered sea shells) has been used with exquisite effect to cover the base of carved wood. The carefully sewn costume—both inner and outer garments—is made of traditional fabrics. The shuttlecock in the left hand and the battledore under the right arm symbolize the traditional Japanese New Year's game. On pages 206–7, Hirata works in his Tokyo studio, putting the finishing touches to a rather stylized doll in voluminous Kabuki costume. Page 208 pictures a touching aspect of his work, for here, at the request of the bereaved parents, he is carving a doll to represent a small boy who was killed in a traffic accident. The snapshots at lower right serve as his guide. The tools on page 209 are only part of a much larger assortment, but they symbolize quite adequately the intricacy and precision of Hirata's work.

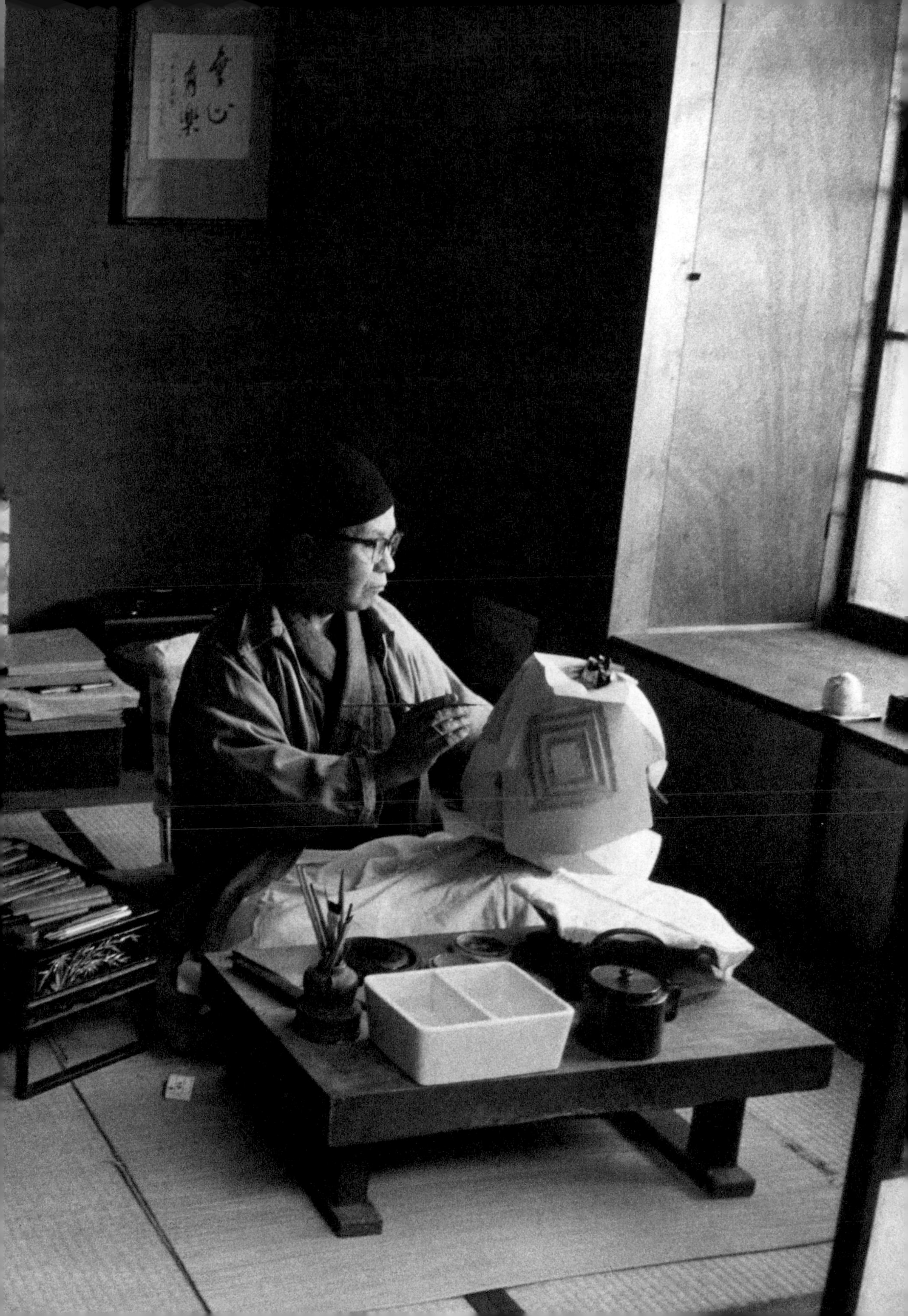

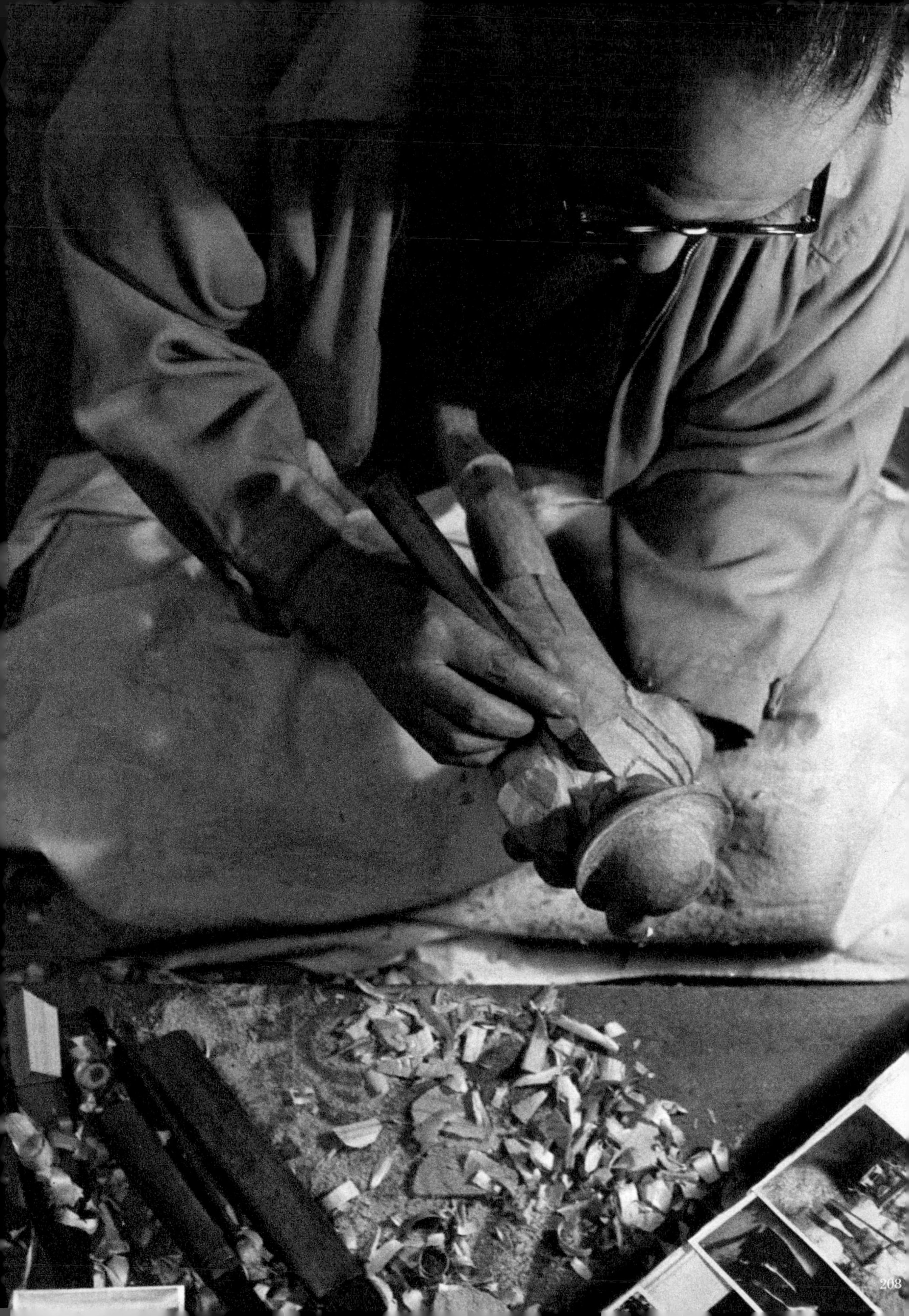

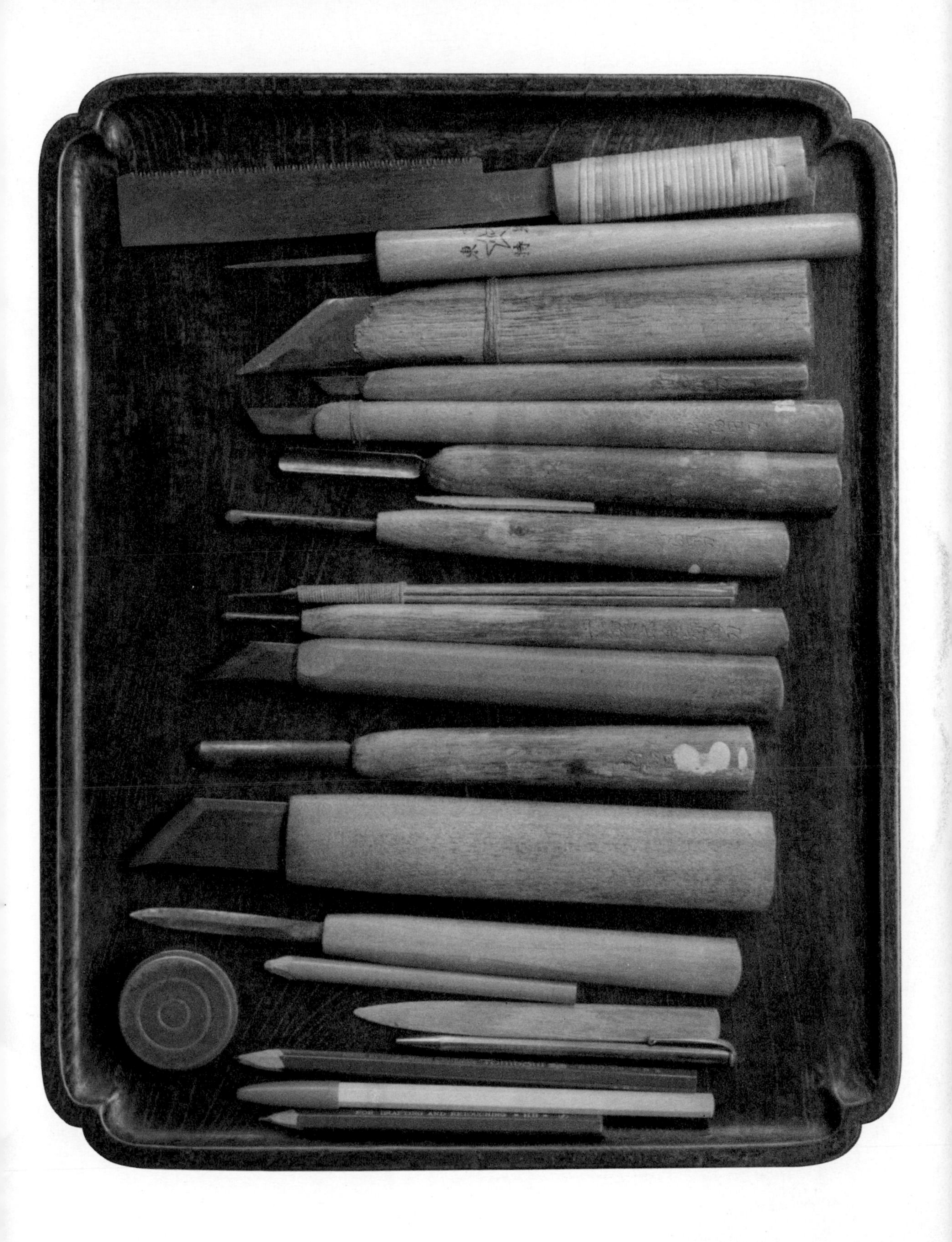

堀柳女

RYUJO HORI

Romanticist of the Costume Doll

Ryujo Hori came to her career as a dollmaker after some years of study under masters of painting, sculpture, and Japanese poetry. Her interest in art and literature has always been a consuming one, and it is reflected in her work. At first she set out to be a painter, but art in two dimensions was somehow unsatisfying, and after some experimenting she turned to the making of dolls. It was soon clear that she had found the right medium to express her remarkable talent. Perhaps it was not entirely fortuitous that two of her teachers of dollmaking were Goyo Hirata (pages 204–9) and Juzo Kagoshima (pages 216–23), both of whom were to become living national treasures. She herself achieved this honor in 1955, at the same time that it was given to Hirata.

Miss Hori is not satisfied to dress her dolls in fabrics made by other craftsmen, regardless of how historically authentic or technically excellent they may be. She weaves her own cloth, dyes it with her own dyes, and sews the costumes herself. Her studies of textiles and costume history have been exhaustive, and she continues them with diligence. Reading and traveling are two of her major occupations when she is not making dolls, and both of these are used to enhance the effectiveness of her art. "No knowledge gained in this way is wasted," she says. "Sooner or later it can be put to use." And then, speaking of her dolls, she says: "What is essential is an element of wonder and surprise. The artist must first of all cultivate it in himself, but he must also express it in everything he creates."

✦

The doll of carved wood on the opposite page is named Toro, which might be translated as "quietness." It represents a lady of ancient times in court dress copied from Chinese styles. The head, the headdress, and the body are painted, but the costume is of textiles made by the artist herself. Like the doll on page 215, this one is owned by the National Commission for the Protection of Cultural Properties. On pages 212–13, Ryujo Hori, in her Tokyo studio, begins the carving of a doll from a single block of wood. Her tools, of which a sample assortment appears on page 214, form an impressive collection and at the same time testify to the extreme delicacy of her work. The doll on page 215, again a figure in ancient court costume, is named not for a person but for the object it holds: Old Mirror. This is a typical Hori touch, and it is meant to enhance the poetic quality of the doll itself.

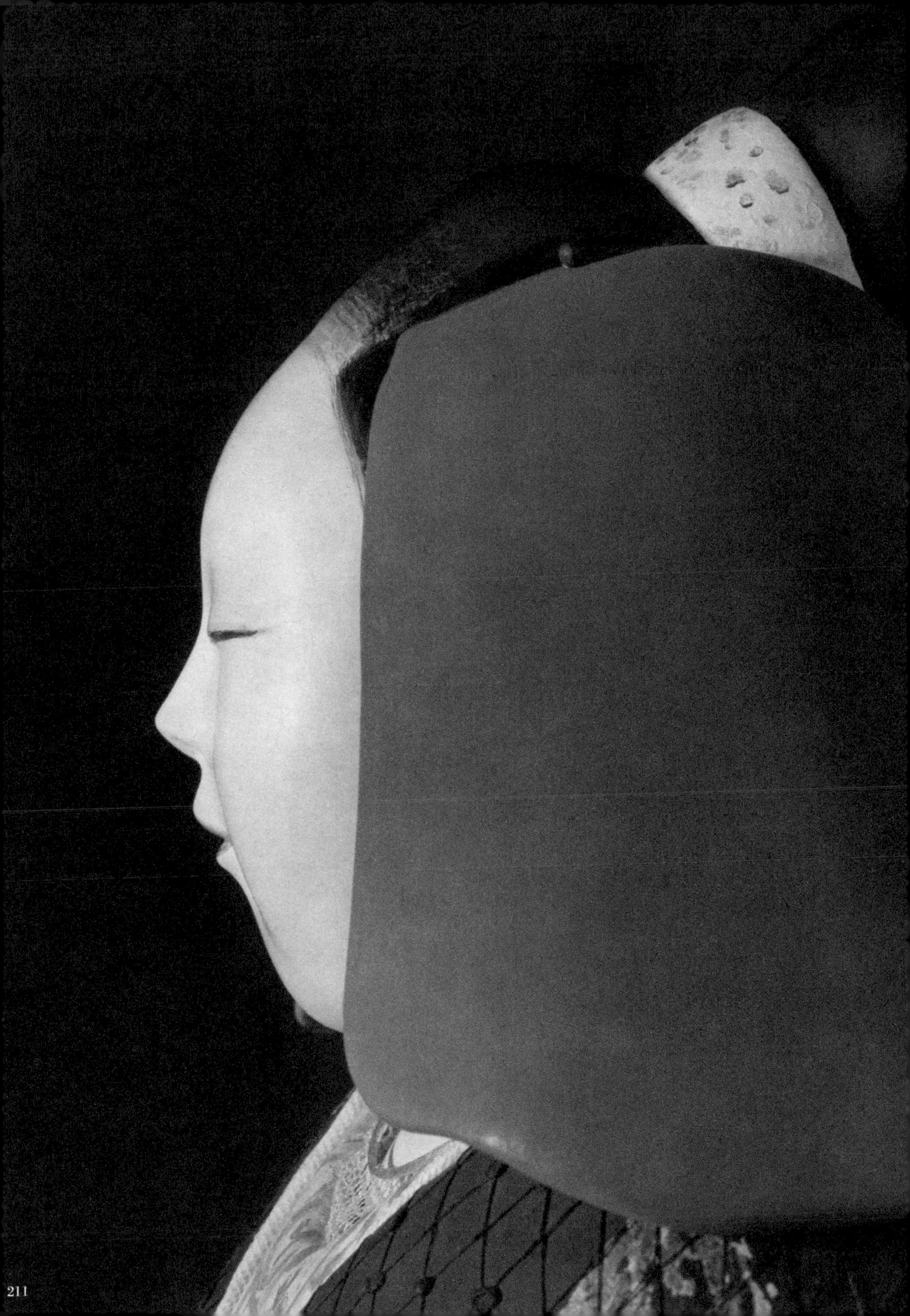

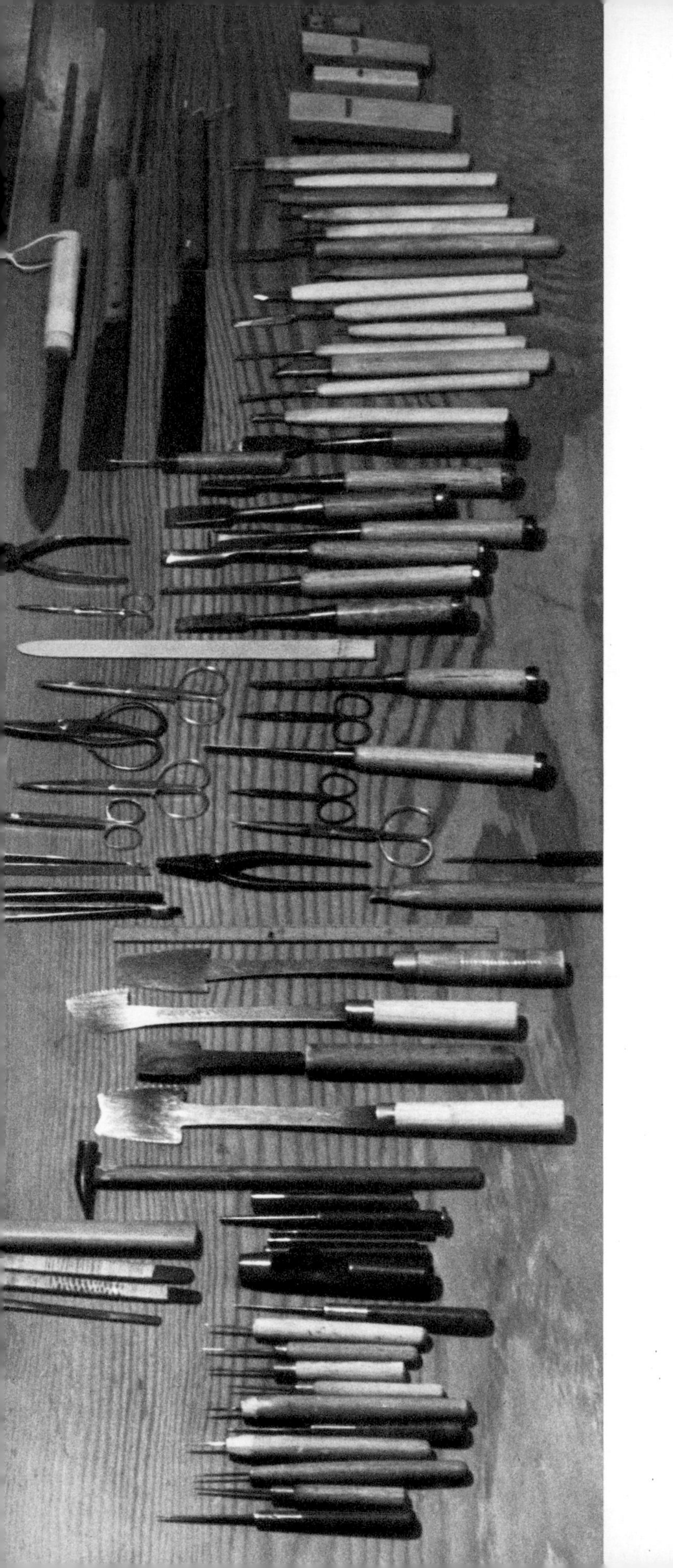

鹿児島寿蔵

JUZO KAGOSHIMA

Master of the Molded-Paper Doll

The craft of making dolls of molded paper has a long tradition in Japan, and Juzo Kagoshima, leading modern master of its techniques, has refined it into an art. Kagoshima was born in Hakata, in Kyushu, and he began his career by learning to make the plaster character dolls for which the city is famous. But the making of Hakata dolls is a mass-production enterprise with no real attractions for the creative artist, and at twenty-two Kagoshima went to Tokyo, where be became fascinated with the technique of the molded-paper doll. It was not long before he had mastered it and added refinements of his own.

To make the material from which he molds his dolls, Kagoshima uses the fibers of two plants much favored in traditional Japanese papermaking: *kozo* (paper mulberry) and *mitsumata* (edgeworthia). These are mixed with gelatin and pounded in a mortar to make a smooth paste. After the basic form of the doll has been molded from this mixture, he begins to paste it over with tiny pieces of dyed paper to produce the color effects. As the work proceeds, the surface is polished from time to time to give it a soft luster. Since the technique is quite complicated, Kagoshima makes only a small number of dolls each year.

Kagoshima is sharply critical of his own work. "The older I get," he says, "the more superficial my dolls seem to become. Because they are dolls, they have a tendency to become conventional, and this I must guard against."

In addition to being a noted dollmaker, Kagoshima is a poet of some renown. Translations of Japanese poetry are never more than approximations at best, but the following at least expresses the thought in one of his poems about dolls. "In this complex world I devote myself to the making of dolls, hoping that they may turn out to be gentle and contented."

✦

On the facing page, Kagoshima is at work on a molded-paper doll with the intriguing name of Star of the Silk Road. The figure represents a Chinese of ancient times—the age in which East and West exchanged products by way of the route across Asia known as the Silk Road. Pages 218–19 show the process of pasting tiny pieces of colored paper on the molded doll. The figure represents a Japanese boy of very early times in a costume of Chinese inspiration. The photograph on pages 220–21 is meant to suggest the mood inspired by the name of the doll itself: Dreams of the Southern Sea. Here the figure is that of a woman in ancient Japanese costume copied from Chinese styles. The delightful dolls on pages 222–23, to which Kagoshima has given the name of Young Craftsmen, were made after he had watched repair work on the Nara-period treasures of the Shoso-in. The costumes are those of the Nara period, and the dolls are meant to evoke the spirit of that distant age.

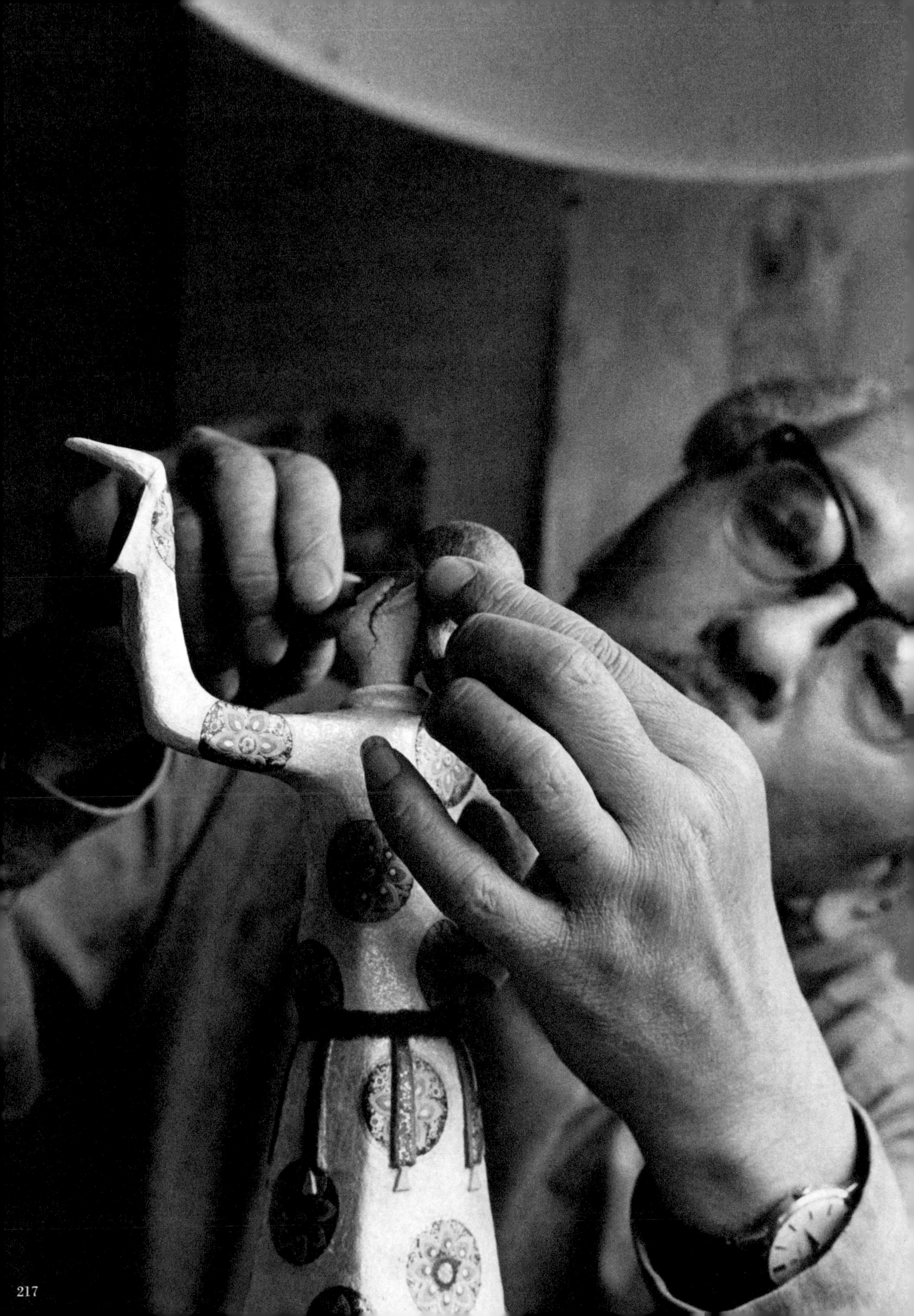

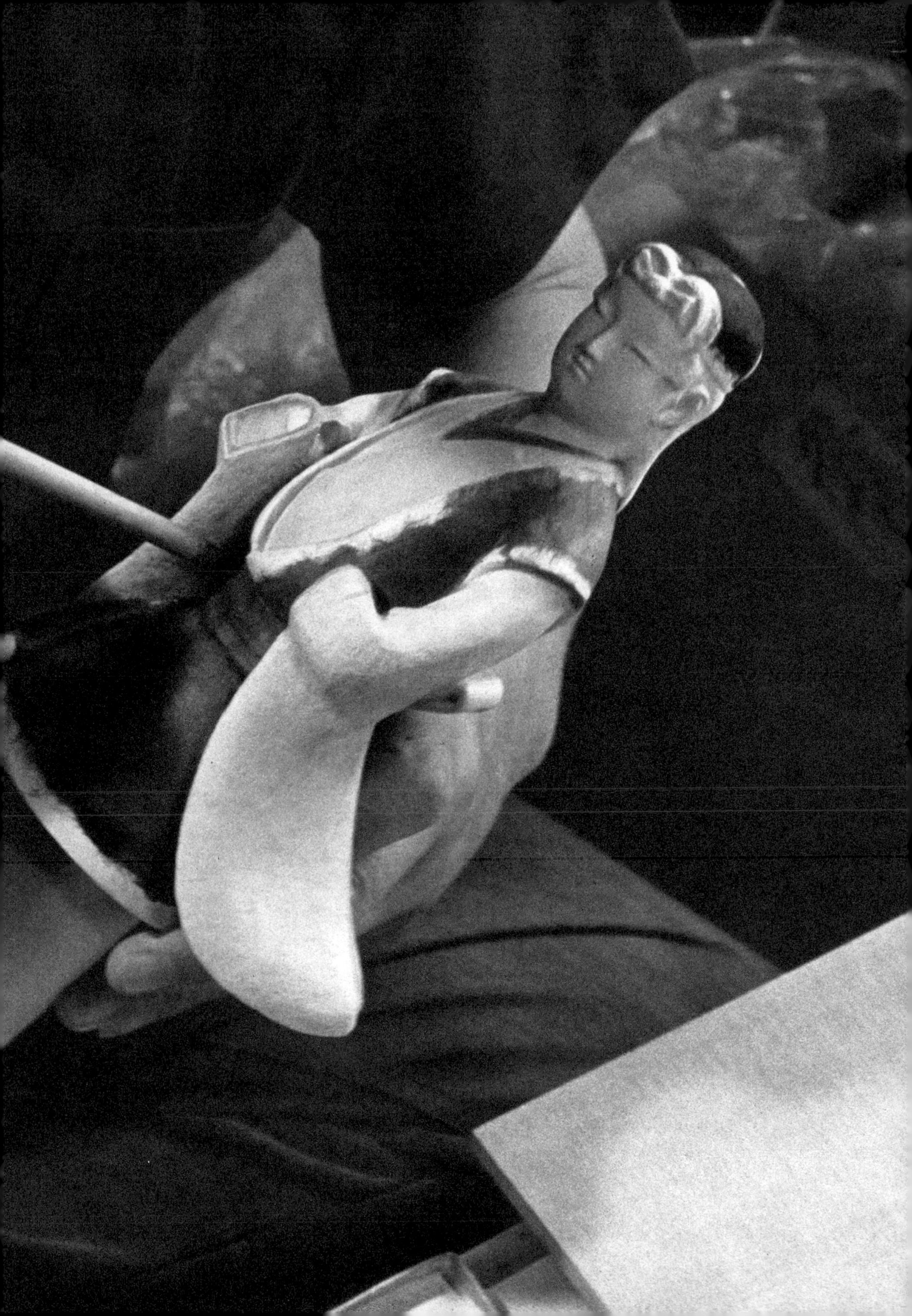

PHOTOGRAPHER'S NOTE

This book has been a long time in the making, but I do not regret a single hour of the hundreds that I had to spend in obtaining the photographs I wanted. In more ways than one, though, I was working against time. The living national treasures among Japan's traditional craftsmen are no less mortal than the rest of us, and some of them are people of great age. This fact in itself gave me a sense of urgency, but there was also the thought that in a number of cases the craft would inevitably disappear with the craftsman.

As readers of the book will have noted, a number of the craftsmen portrayed here are the very last of their line and will have no successors. Since the end of the Pacific War in 1945, young Japanese have been increasingly reluctant to take up traditional crafts, for they see no future in such occupations, and they live in a world where long apprenticeship offers no attractions at all. The tempo of life in Japan today—to say nothing of current ideas about economic values—does not encourage the learning of crafts for reasons of tradition alone. In a word, then, I felt that I must record these traditional crafts before they disappeared forever.

It may interest the reader to have some general idea of the effort that went into the book—not that I am seeking commendation for myself and those who helped me (we do not need it, for the book itself is what really matters)—but that he may know how rewarding, and sometimes difficult, the experience was. I shall refrain here from mentioning any of the living national treasures by name, since part of what I have to say might be embarrassing to some of them, although certainly none of it will make them seem less human. Let me deal with a few typical difficulties first.

To begin with, it required an exchange of more than four hundred letters with these thirty-three men and women before arrangements for visiting them could be completed. In one case the correspondence went on for over a year. Some made appointments with no reluctance or delay; others declined outright on first approach and had to be persuaded through patient diplomacy. Still others, when my assistants and I visited them, showed no hesitation at all in giving us detailed advice as to how we should go about our work. In one instance we undertook a six-hour drive from Tokyo for an interview and a photographing session that lasted no more than fifteen minutes. That was all the craftsman would grant, and it hardly made our mission easier, even though we could understand his jealousy of his time. Another excursion required two days of mountain climbing in central Japan with a carload of equipment.

The case of the craftsman who yielded only after more than a year of correspondence (and a number of telephone calls) was perhaps the most interesting of all. He eventually told me that he was much impressed by the patient and untiring endeavors of the young lady who handled all this for me and that this was his reason for finally agreeing to be photographed. He thought the young lady was my wife, and this may have had something to do with his eventual surrender. While this campaign by mail and phone was in progress, I went repeatedly to the bar in Tokyo where he was said to be a frequent visitor, but he just as repeatedly stayed away, and my hope of striking up an acquaintance with him came to nothing. There was an advantage in this, however, for I learned a good deal about him from the people in the bar, and when we finally met I had the feeling that we had known each other for years. Oddly enough, after our first encounter he allowed me to meet him almost whenever and wherever I wished.

But if some of the living national treasures were jealous of their privacy and their time—and justifiably so, let me say—others were more than generous, and here the rewards of the experience came in. Once we had become acquainted with them, my staff and I were often invited to stay for dinner and meet the family, and a genuine friendship developed. More than that, there was the reward of exchanging ideas and opinions with these craftsmen and getting to know them in their roles as living national treasures. Quite often, in the midst of the quiet sounds of camera and chisel or loom or potter's wheel, we established a most pleasant rapport. The craftsmen were no longer merely names to us, and we felt ourselves to be more than just a crew of cameramen who had come to record a few pages of living history.

I am greatly indebted to the many people who helped to make this book a reality. It is impossible to name all of them here, and since I have no wish to make a selection that would run the risk of being invidious, I shall say quite simply that I offer to all of them my heartfelt gratitude and that I am particularly grateful to my cooperative staff. At the same time, I must express my deep regret that I am unable to show this book to the man who first encouraged me in the project and undertook the plans for publication of the original Japanese edition. He was Masao Oshita, president of the publishing house of Bijutsu Shuppan-sha, who lost his life in a plane crash in Japan in February 1966. It would mean a great deal to me to know that he liked the book.

TSUNE SUGIMURA

BRIEF BIOGRAPHIES

ARAKAWA, TOYOZO (pages 12–17). Potter. Born March 21, 1894, in Tajimi, Gifu Prefecture. Present residence: Kuguri, Kani-machi, Gifu Prefecture. Student of ceramic art under Tozan Miyanaga and Rosanjin Kitaoji. Designated a living national treasure in 1955 for his Shino and Black Seto ware.

CHIBA, AYANO (pages 108–15). Dyer and weaver. Born November 14, 1889, in Miyagi Prefecture. Present residence: Kurikoma-machi, Miyagi Prefecture. Designated a living national treasure in 1955 for her indigo dyeing.

FUKAMI, JUSUKE (pages 54–59). Weaver. Born March 16, 1885, in Kyoto, representing thirteenth generation of famous textile house of Matsubaya. Present residence: Kyoto. Designated a living national treasure in 1956 for his *karagumi:* weaving of decorative sashes in ancient style. Awarded Japan Kiwanis Club prize in 1966 for the same accomplishment.

HAMADA, SHOJI (pages 24–34). Potter. Born December 9, 1894, in Kawasaki, Kanagawa Prefecture. Present residence: Mashiko-machi, Tochigi Prefecture. Leader, with the late Soetsu Yanagi, in Japanese folk-art movement. Present director of Nihon Mingeikan (Japan Folk Art Museum), Tokyo. Designated a living national treasure in 1955 for his folk pottery.

HIRATA, GOYO (pages 204–9). Dollmaker. Born November 25, 1903, in Tokyo. Present residence: same. Leader of Yomonkai, a group of traditional dollmakers. Designated a living national treasure in 1955 for his costume dolls of carved wood.

HORI, RYUJO (pages 210–15). Dollmaker. Born August 25, 1897, in Tokyo, as Matsue Yamada. Present residence: Tokyo. Studied under four masters, including Goyo Hirata and Juzo Kagoshima (both living national treasures). Designated a living national treasure in 1955 for her costume dolls of carved wood.

ISHIGURO, MUNEMARO (pages 6–11). Potter. Born April 14, 1893, in Niihama, Toyama Prefecture. Present residence: Yase, Kyoto. Designated a living national treasure in 1955 for his iron-glazed ceramics.

JONOKUCHI, MIE (pages 91, 104–6). Stencil technician. Born January 2, 1917, in Suzuka, Mie Prefecture. Present residence: same. Designated a living national treasure in 1955 for her *ito-ire:* strengthening of paper stencils for textiles by pasting them over with fine silk thread.

KAGOSHIMA, JUZO (pages 216–23). Dollmaker. Born December 10, 1898, in Hakata, Fukuoka Prefecture, Kyushu. Present residence: Tokyo. Designated a living national treasure in 1961 for his molded-paper dolls. Also well known as a poet.

KANESHIGE, TOYO (pages 18–23). Potter. Born January 3, 1896, in Bizen-machi, Okayama Prefecture. Died at Okayama City, November 5, 1967. Designated a living national treasure in 1956 for his Bizen ware.

KATO, HAJIME (pages 36–42). Potter. Born March 7, 1900, in Seto, Aichi Prefecture. Present residence: Yokohama. Professor at Tokyo University of Arts. Designated a living national treasure in 1961 for his color-decorated ceramics.

KIMURA, UZAN (pages 60–65). Dyer. Born February 21, 1891, in Kanazawa, Ishikawa Prefecture. Present residence: same. Former teacher of dyeing at Ishikawa Prefectural Industrial

Arts School. Designated a living national treasure in 1955 for his Kaga *yuzen:* paste-resist dyeing in traditional Kaga style.

KITAGAWA, HEIRO (pages 48–53). Weaver. Born July 15, 1898, in Kyoto, representing seventeenth generation of famous textile house of Tawaraya. Present residence: Kyoto. Designated a living national treasure in 1956 for his *ra* (gauze-weave silk in ancient style) and in 1961 for his *yusoku orimono* (fabrics in the styles of the Nara and Heian periods).

KODA, EISUKE (pages 116–20). Dyer and weaver. Born July 10, 1902, in Sendai, Miyagi Prefecture. Present residence: same. Designated a living national treasure in 1956 for his fabrics in "exquisite Sendai weave."

KODAMA, HIROSHI (pages 91, 100–101). Stencilmaker. Born October 13, 1907, in Suzuka, Mie Prefecture. Present residence: same. Designated a living national treasure in 1955 for his fine-line textile stencils in striped patterns.

MAE, TAIHO (pages 146–50). Lacquer artist. Born November 10, 1890, in Wajima, Ishikawa Prefecture. Present residence: same. Designated a living national treasure in 1955 for his gold-inlayed lacquer ware.

MATSUDA, GONROKU (pages 126–31). Lacquer artist. Born April 20, 1896, in Kanazawa, Ishikawa Prefecture. Present residence: Tokyo. Former teacher at Tokyo University of Arts. Leader in promotion of traditional handicraft arts. Designated a living national treasure in 1955 for his gold-decorated lacquer ware in *maki-e* (sown picture) style.

MIYAIRI, AKIHIRA (pages 168–76). Swordsmith. Born March 17, 1913, in Sakaki-machi, Nagano Prefecture, to a swordmaking family of long history. Present residence: Sakaki-machi, Nagano Prefecture. Frequent winner of prizes for swordmaking; maker of swords for presentation to Grand Shrine of Ise and Yasukuni Shrine. Designated a living national treasure in 1963 for his swords in traditional Japanese style.

MORIGUCHI, KAKO (pages 86–89). Dyer. Born December 10, 1909, in Kyoto, as Heishichiro Moriguchi. Present residence: Kyoto. Designated a living national treasure in 1967 for his *yuzen makinori:* paste-resist dyeing in pointillist style.

NAGANO, TETSUSHI (pages 178–85). Maker of iron teakettles. Born October 28, 1901, in Nagoya. Present residence: Tokyo. Foundry: Yamagata City, Yamagata Prefecture. Designated a living national treasure in 1963 for his iron kettles for tea-ceremony use.

NAKAJIMA, HIDEKICHI (pages 91, 102–3). Stencilmaker. Born September 4, 1883, in Suzuka, Mie Prefecture. Present residence: same. Designated a living national treasure in 1955 for his textile stencils in traditional small patterns.

NAKAMURA, KATSUMA (pages 66–73). Dyer. Born September 18, 1894, in Iwate Prefecture. Present residence: Chofu, Tokyo. Designated a living national treasure in 1955 for his *yuzen* (paste-resist) dyeing in Edo style.

NAKAMURA, YUJIRO (pages 90, 94–97). Stencilmaker. Born September 20, 1902, in Suzuka, Mie Prefecture. Present residence: same. Designated a living national treasure in 1955 for his textile stencils in allover geometric patterns.

NAMBU, YOSHIMATSU (pages 90, 92–93). Stencilmaker. Born September 20, 1894, in Suzuka, Mie Prefecture. Present residence: same. Designated a living national treasure in 1955 for his floral-patterned textile stencils in *tsukibori* (pierced) style.

OTOMARU, KODO (pages 140–45). Lacquer artist. Born June 15, 1898, in Takamatsu, Kagawa Prefecture, Shikoku. Present residence: Tokyo. Designated a living national treasure in 1955 for his multicolored carved lacquer ware.

ROKUTANI, BAIKEN (pages 90, 98–99). Stencilmaker. Born February 15, 1907, in Suzuka, Mie Prefecture. Present residence: same. Designated a living national treasure in 1955 for his textile stencils in allover geometric patterns.

SERIZAWA, KEISUKE (pages 74–79). Stencilmaker and dyer. Born May 13, 1895, in Shizuoka City, Shizuoka Prefecture. Present residence: Tokyo. Leader, along with potter Shoji Hamada and the late Soetsu Yanagi, in Japanese folk-art movement. Designated a living national treasure in 1956 for his stencil dyeing of textiles and papers.

SHIMIZU, KOTARO (pages 80–85). Dyer. Born January 28, 1897, in Tokyo. Present residence: same. Designated a living national treasure in 1955 for his stencil-dyed textiles in repeat patterns.

SHONO, SHOUNSAI (pages 194–98). Bamboo artist. Born September 10, 1904, in Beppu, Oita Prefecture, Kyushu, as Akihira Shono. Present residence: Beppu. Designated a living national treasure in 1967 for his bamboo work.

TAKAHASHI, SADATSUGU (pages 156–61). Swordsmith. Born April 14, 1902, in Saijo, Ehime Prefecture, Shikoku, as Kin'ichi Takahashi. Honorary title as swordsmith: Ryusen. Present residence: Matsuyama, Ehime Prefecture. Designated a living national treasure in 1955 for his swords in traditional Japanese style.

TAKAMURA, TOYOCHIKA (pages 186–90). Metalcaster. Born July 1, 1890, in Tokyo, as son of celebrated sculptor Koun Takamura. Present residence: Tokyo. Former teacher at Tokyo University of Arts. Designated a living national treasure in 1964 for his cast-metal art objects in lost-wax technique. Also well known as a poet.

TAKANO, SHOZAN (pages 132–39). Lacquer artist. Born May 2, 1889, in Kumamoto Prefecture, Kyushu. Present residence: Tokyo. Designated a living national treasure in 1955 for his gold-decorated lacquer ware in *maki-e* (sown picture) style.

YONEMITSU, TAHEI (pages 162–67). Maker of metal sword guards. Born May 1, 1888, in Kumamoto City, Kumamoto Prefecture, Kyushu. Present residence: same. Designated a living national treasure in 1965 for his damascene and openwork in Higo style: the traditional style of the region where he works.

The "weathermark" identifies this book as having been planned, designed, ana produced by John Weatherhill, Inc., 7-6-13 Roppongi, Minato-ku, Tokyo, in collaboration with Bijutsu Shuppan-sha, Tokyo, the publishers of the Japanese edition. Layout of plates by Bijutsu Shuppan-sha. Book design and typography by Meredith Weatherby and Miriam F. Yamaguchi. Text composed and printed by Kenkyusha, Tokyo. Color and gravure plates engraved and printed by Inshokan, Tokyo. Bound at the Makoto Binderies, Tokyo. The main text is set in 11-point Monotype Baskerville, with hand-set Bulmer for display.

Actual-size photograph of a late-19th-century stencil employing the same *shimabori* technique used by Hiroshi Kodama (pp. 100 -1) and strengthened with silk threads in the way used by Mie Jonokuchi (pp. 104-6). This particular stencil, with